TREK

THE MAKING OF THE MOVIES

BY JAMES VAN HISE

Library of Congress Cataloging-in-Publication Data
James Van Hise, 1949—
    Trek: The Making of the Movies

    1. Trek: The Making of the Movies (popular culture)
 I. Title

Published by Pioneer Books, Inc., 5715 N. Balsam Rd., Las Vegas, NV, 89130.

First Printing, 1992

JAMES VAN HISE writes about film, television and comic book history. He has written numerous books on these subjects, including BAT-MANIA, 25th ANNIVERSARY TREK TRIBUTE BOOK, STEPHEN KING & CLIVE BARKER: THE ILLUSTRATED GUIDE TO THE MASTERS OF THE MACABRE, CHEERS and HOW TO DRAW ART FOR COMIC BOOKS: LESSONS FROM THE MASTERS. He is the publisher of MIDNIGHT GRAFFITI, in which he has run previously unpublished stories by Stephen King and Harlan Ellison. Van Hise resides in San Diego along with his wife, horses and various other animals and writes comic books.

TREK: THE MAKING OF THE MOVIES

THE MAKING OF THE MOVIES

On the morning of December 7, 1979, I was in one of many lines threading around the corner of major movie theaters all over the country *Star Trek: The Motion Picture* had come to town. It turned out to be a mixed blessing, but the film had its moments. It played theaters for several months (a rarity for any film these days) and it gave fans a lot to talk and argue about.

Two and a half years later a lot of arguing preceded the release of the next *Star Trek* film. *The Wrath of Khan,* as most everyone knew by June 1982, featured the death of Mr. Spock. When had anyone ever made such a fuss over the death of an imaginary character before? But those who condemned the film sight unseen found they liked it after all—and went back to see it several more times.

By the time *The Search For Spock* was released in 1984, I was writing about films for *Enterprise Incidents* and saw the film at a special screening in Los Angeles which included other members of the press, as well as guys like DeForest Kelley. Seeing the Enterprise blow up from a balcony seat is a rare privilege. I was impressed.

The Voyage Home was viewed in November 1986 at a large screening room on the Paramount lot with many others in the audience, including Walter Koenig, James Doohan and Nicholas Meyer. I overheard Meyer tell his date, "I wrote all the funny stuff. Harve Bennett can't write humor." It was a nice movie, even if the theme sounded like Christmas music.

I saw *Star Trek V* among civilians again. It wasn't bad; certainly not as bad as some made it out to be. Sure, it has some cheesy special effects there at the end, but the script wasn't any worse than *Star Trek III* or *IV*. I could have lived without seeing Scotty knock himself out on an overhead beam (that's called stretching for a joke) and his ill-advised pawing of Uhura, but none of the films are perfect.

The Undiscovered Country is very entertaining, but seems a bit too slick and remote to me. I never really got involved. Did you have any doubts that Kirk and McCoy would escape from the prison planet? That went on a bit long considering nothing about it was ever in doubt. Still, it was fun, but fell a bit short of being dramatic. The various mysteries in it were what mostly fueled the plot. I also doubt this will be the last voyage of Kirk and company. Considering how bland and undynamic most of the characters on *The Next Generation* are.

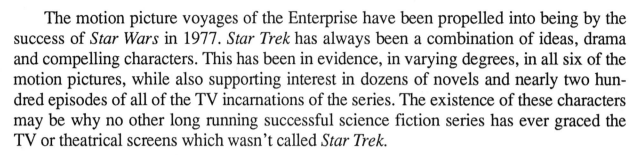

The motion picture voyages of the Enterprise have been propelled into being by the success of *Star Wars* in 1977. *Star Trek* has always been a combination of ideas, drama and compelling characters. This has been in evidence, in varying degrees, in all six of the motion pictures, while also supporting interest in dozens of novels and nearly two hundred episodes of all of the TV incarnations of the series. The existence of these characters may be why no other long running successful science fiction series has ever graced the TV or theatrical screens which wasn't called *Star Trek*.

—JAMES VAN HISE, JAN 1992

—JAMES VAN HISE

Discussions between Paramount and Gene Roddenberry over a Star Trek revival started as early as 1973, with talk about a motion picture beginning in 1975. However, it would be 1976 before actual money was spent towards a revival, and 1979 before the fans saw it come to life on theatre screens.

ONE: THE MOTION PICTURE

"Why are we now traveling into space? Why, indeed, did we trouble to look past the next mountain? Our prime obligation to ourselves is to make the unknown known. We are on a journey to keep an appointment with whatever we are." —Gene Roddenberry

When *Star Trek: The Motion Picture* was released in 1979, the tag line in the advertisement was, "The Human Adventure Is Just Beginning." Getting the movie to the screen was an adventure almost on the same scale as what was finally presented on the screen.

The quote by Gene Roddenberry at the beginning of this chapter comes from a newsletter about the film issued by Paramount Pictures in the summer of 1979. Written by an unnamed Paramount functionary, the newsletter began by introducing Roddenberry who, while having been given the cold shoulder by the studio for several years after the cancellation of *Star Trek* in 1969, was suddenly in Paramount's good graces again. The newsletter states, "Gene Roddenberry is the producer of Paramount's new multi-million dollar space adventure drama *Star Trek: The Motion Picture*. For him, the film culminates a 14 year labor of love that began in 1964 when he created the *Star Trek* TV series. After two pilots had been made, the show began its three-year run on NBC in 1966 with Roddenberry producing. After being cancelled by the network and placed in syndication throughout the world in 1970, the series inspired an unprecedented show business phenomenon that continues to this day."

Just as the winds of change could blow Roddenberry back into the good graces of Paramount, they could just as quickly change direction, as the producer would eventually learn.

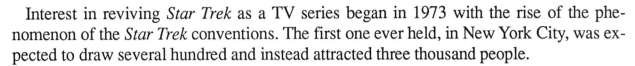

Interest in reviving *Star Trek* as a TV series began in 1973 with the rise of the phenomenon of the *Star Trek* conventions. The first one ever held, in New York City, was expected to draw several hundred and instead attracted three thousand people.

A year after the cancellation of *Star Trek*, NBC began using an additional system for calculating ratings which is called demographics. Demographics measures the type of people who watched a show. It was determined in 1970 that the audience for *Star Trek* achieved perfect demographics, which would have made it extremely attractive to sponsors. Roddenberry observed that had demographics come in a year earlier or had *Star Trek* lasted a year longer, the series could have gone on for ten years with its demographics.

NBC approached Roddenberry about reviving *Star Trek* in 1973, but they wanted him to produce a new pilot episode. Roddenberry refused, stating, "We did 79 pilots! We don't need to do another one!" But NBC was firm and they parted ways.

What did make it on NBC through Filmation, was a Star Trek cartoon series. Roddenberry had been approached by other animation houses with suggestions to adapt the series into animation, but he had turned them down when their proposals included either making the show "cute" or having our heroes landing on a planet and blasting any alien which had the misfortune of looking like a monster.

Filmation didn't want to tamper with the concept and let Roddenberry produce the series to insure its quality control. A total of twenty-two episodes were produced and the first step on the long road to the return of a live action *Star Trek* had been done. The fact that the animated show included the voices of the original cast made it indeed an official part of the canon.

The reception of the *Star Trek* animated series, and the ongoing and increasing popularity of the *Star Trek* conventions, brought Paramount back into the picture again. They negotiated with Roddenberry for a year and a half before giving him an office on the studio lot in May of 1975, and committing $3 million for a moderately sized motion picture. Roddenberry was given the same offices he'd used in the sixties for the TV series and he proceeded to begin work writing the screenplay for what was then called *Star Trek II*, which Paramount hoped to produce and get into theaters by the end of that same year. It didn't work out quite that way.

The script Roddenberry wrote is the notorious "*Star Trek* meets God" storyline. The "God" of the storyline was a being from another dimension who was referred to as the "deceiver." The script postulated that the God and Satan of the Bible were actually inversions of the truth. The story ended with Kirk defeating "God" and upon returning to Earth finding that he and his crew have gone back in time to the end of their five year mission and regained their youth.

While Paramount rejected this storyline as being too controversial, certain scenes and

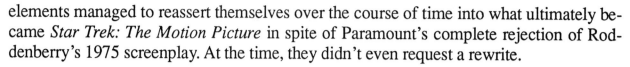

elements managed to reassert themselves over the course of time into what ultimately became *Star Trek: The Motion Picture* in spite of Paramount's complete rejection of Roddenberry's 1975 screenplay. At the time, they didn't even request a rewrite.

Paramount delayed the film and invited other writers experienced in science fiction to come in and pitch their ideas. This included writers who'd previously written for the series, such as John D.F. Black, Ted Sturgeon and Harlan Ellison. Whatever Paramount was looking for, the ideas suggested by these writers didn't hit the mark.

Roddenberry was not idle during this time as he sat down with writer Jon Povill (who later became the Associate Producer of ST-TMP) and wrote a time travel story in which history is changed and Capt. Kirk has to set events back on the right track. This is the famous story rumored to have Kirk required to go back in time and kill JFK after the President's life is saved and history is changed because of it. Roddenberry later denied that this specific event was in the story.

On January 21, 1976, Roddenberry circulated a memo to all interested parties stating that Paramount was still serious about producing a movie and had given him a start date for production of July 15, 1976. Said Roddenberry, "In eight months it's gone from casual disinterest to pressing enthusiasm. We don't have a script yet but then there are a lot of people with scripts who don't have a start date."

In July, no script was in hand and no new writer had been approved. But Paramount was still keeping the project alive and upped the budget into the $6 to $8 million range and assigned Jerry Isenberg as executive producer. Jon Povill was hired as Isenberg's assistant and his first assignment was to compile a list of possible writers. This list included Robert Towne, Francis Ford Coppola, George Lucas (who was then directing a film in England called *Star Wars*), Robert Bloch, Paddy Chayefsky and Carl Gottlieb (who was hot then due to his screenplay for *Jaws*). There were 34 names on the list and none of them were chosen. Jon Povill had also compiled a list for Gene of possible directors, which included Steven Spielberg, William Friedkin, George Roy Hill, Norman Jewison, George Lucas, Francis Coppola and Robert Wise. This list proved to have more foresight than the writer's list.

But none of them were available at the time, and so Phil Kaufman was hired to direct *Star Trek II*. Two British screenwriters, Allan Scott and Chris Bryant, were hired to write a screenplay even though they had no experience writing science fiction. Still, Roddenberry had been impressed with the questions they asked and believed they had the right stuff.

That interest in *Star Trek* continued to be unflagging was proven in 1976 when 400,000 letters flooded the White House urging that the first space shuttle be named Enterprise. It was and the cast of *Star Trek* went to Palmdale, California on September 17, 1976 for the rolling out ceremony of the newly christened space shuttle. Enthusiasm over this feat was

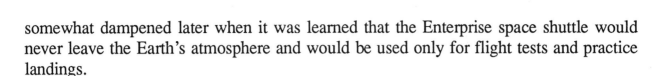

somewhat dampened later when it was learned that the Enterprise space shuttle would never leave the Earth's atmosphere and would be used only for flight tests and practice landings.

Bryant and Scott turned in their story outline for a *Star Trek* movie on October 8, 1976, which Paramount approved, but they didn't complete a script until March 1, 1977. The script had the Enterprise discovering a hidden planet where Capt. Kirk had vanished three years before. It was altered so much by studio input that it bore little resemblance to the original story outline and now Paramount didn't like it any more!

When Paramount rejected the script and Bryant and Scott returned to England, the rumor mills churned furiously with the word that the movie had been cancelled.

The project was actually in limbo, but it sure seemed like a cancellation to those involved. As Walter Koenig described it later, "We had a party at Bill Shatner's house celebrating the start of the film. That was a Friday. On the next Monday I went in for a costume fitting. By Tuesday the film was dead."

In May 1977 a movie opened called *Star Wars* and suddenly it became clear to anyone and everyone that science fiction was a potentially lucrative film subject. It should be remembered that up until this time there had been no really successful science fiction films in the sixties or seventies. Even Stanley Kubrick's *2001: A Space Odyssey* had cost $10 million to film and took eight years just to break even, despite the wide critical acclaim and massive publicity the film received. *Planet Of The Apes* (and its series of increasingly low budget sequels) had actually been more profitable, but weren't close to blockbusters.

In June 1977, when people were lining up around the block to see *Star Wars*, I attended a convention in Houston, Texas where George Takei was a guest. At one point a handful of us were sitting around talking to George and he revealed that he didn't believe that Paramount had ever been serious about making a *Star Trek* film. He thought at the time that all of Paramount's talk about a film was just so much publicity to maintain interest in the syndication of the TV series. The fact that talk about a film had dragged on for two years without any participation of the actors no doubt colored his perceptions at the time. But this would soon change.

The wheels of progress grind slowly and even while *Star Wars* was just beginning to make an impression, Paramount issued a publicity release on June 17, 1977 about something they called *Star Trek: Phase II*. This was for a new TV series which would launch a fourth network Paramount intended to create in competition with the three majors: ABC, NBC & CBS. It was not unlike what 20th Century Fox succeeded in doing a decade later with the Fox Network.

Richard Frank, vice president of Paramount Pictures Corporation stated in the press release, "*Star Trek* will be the foundation for the new Paramount Television Service. It rep-

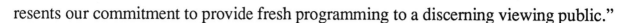

resents our commitment to provide fresh programming to a discerning viewing public."

Production was slated to begin in the fall and the actors were contacted to begin contract negotiations. George Takei spoke a tad too soon.

By June 17, 1977, while *Star Wars* was doing well, it was only just beginning to open all across the country. While it opened in major cities on May 25, 1977, many other cities, even centers as large as Miami, Florida, didn't get the film until 3 weeks later. So it wasn't clear until a month later that *Star Wars* wasn't just doing well, it was a blockbuster bigger than *Jaws* and business was not dropping off as it broke the $100 million mark and kept on going. The perception of science fiction wasn't just changing, it was undergoing a complete transformation.

Meanwhile, Paramount wanted *Star Trek II* (the new name of the TV series, the Phase part having been dropped) to begin production by late fall for a scheduled premiere of spring 1978. Robert Goodwin and Harold Livingston were hired as co-producers and Gene Roddenberry busily assembled a creative staff. Harold Livingston is a writer with a long list of credits. An author of seven books up to that time, he'd also written scripts for such films as *Escape From Mindano* and *The Soul Of Nigger Charlie,* as well as one hundred television scripts. Livingston's book *Coasts Of The Earth* won the Houghton Mifflin Fellowship Award.

Construction on the sets of the new Enterprise began on stage 9 on the Paramount backlot on July 25, 1977. The time of talk had passed and the time of action had arrived. Joe Jennings was hired as art director and Matt Jeffries, who had worked with Roddenberry to design the Enterprise back in 1965 was also on hand to serve in the capacity of creative consultant. Soundstages 8, 9 and 10 were assigned to *Star Trek* with stage 9 set aside specifically for Enterprise interiors

Co-producer Harold Livingston began lining up writers for the series scripts as well as working on one himself called "In Thy Image" based on a story by Alan Dean Foster and Gene Roddenberry. This script would serve as the two hour series premiere which would reintroduce *Star Trek* and its new characters. Therein lay the first hitch. Leonard Nimoy would not reprise the role of Spock.

While Nimoy had been initially interested in playing the role for a movie, he was not interested in returning to the weekly grind of a television series after doing three years of the original *Star Trek* and two years of *Mission: Impossible*. A TV movie Nimoy had stared in called *Baffled* had been successful enough for the producers of that film to offer Nimoy the chance to bring it back as a series, but the actor had turned them down flat. The situation with *Star Trek* was more complicated than was let on at the time.

Nimoy had an on-going disagreement with Paramount that had never been settled involving *Star Trek* merchandising. Whenever Spock appeared on a product, the character bore Nimoy's likeness and yet the actor had not received a share of those merchandising monies. This was something which had slipped through the cracks in the sixties and never been rectified.

In fact, it's not common for an actor's face to be used on toys, as any trip through the toy store will prove. Batman toys in 1989 did not look like Michael Keaton, and in fact looked more like Jay Leno. When Marvel Comics produced an adaptation of *Battlestar: Galactica* using actor likenesses, the book had to be redrawn at the last minute due to the lack of permission. Special permissions and extra fees have to be paid to use an actor's likeness, and Nimoy had never had a contract which granted that. But because it had been ongoing for so long, Paramount didn't feel that Nimoy had the right to complain now. Nimoy's dispute with Paramount would not be settled until a year later.

Gene Roddenberry tried without success to get Nimoy to agree to return. Nimoy was not interested in returning to television on a weekly basis, particularly at a time when he was appearing on the Broadway stage in the renowned play "Equus." Nimoy's refusal to participate in *Star Trek* II (as the TV series was still being called) engendered a lot of heated emotions from the fans, and Nimoy received a good bit of critical mail accusing him of trying to "destroy" *Star Trek*.

In an article which appeared in the August 4, 1977 issue of "The Soho Weekly News," Nimoy was quoted as saying, "I have misgivings about not playing Spock. And I have a lot of personal torture about what's going on with that series. It's not easy for me.

"I hate to concern myself with going back to a series nine years after finishing and wonder what am I getting myself into? Is it something we'd really be proud of, or is it simply a rip-off, cash in on the fact that it was just popular because of what we did eight or nine or ten years ago?

"If they do it, it's called *Star Trek* but that doesn't necessarily mean it is *Star Trek*. It all came together and it worked before, but that was in a particular time and a particular place with a particular group of people. You just don't know what will happen this time and there's no way to predict."

Regarding the violent antagonism to his decision not to play Spock in a new weekly series, Nimoy explained, "You can't please everybody, and when you're a public figure, people do develop a proprietary interest. People believe they are responsible for your success. People do believe you owe them the rest of your choices in activity — that you should check with them and make sure it's okay with them to do what you're doing. The irony of it is — and the toughest thing to come to grips with — is that I played a character who said to me, 'An individual should use his life to do whatever he is capable of doing to fulfill himself.' A character who says, 'I refuse to be boxed in by my exoticness,' who says, 'I will do whatever I can with my life.'

"Now, eight or nine years later, Leonard Nimoy is out doing that. And there are people who don't want him to do what Spock says people should do. That's the irony. It really

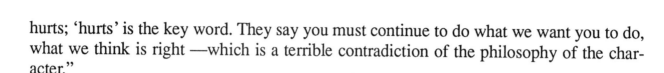

hurts; 'hurts' is the key word. They say you must continue to do what we want you to do, what we think is right —which is a terrible contradiction of the philosophy of the character."

When it became obvious that Gene Roddenberry could not talk Nimoy into joining the cast of *Star Trek II*, he chose the next logical alternative. Rather than recast Spock with a new actor, he created a new Vulcan to fill Spock's position on the Enterprise, Lieutenant Xon.

In the new writer's guide created by Roddenberry, it stated, "Can a twenty-two year-old Vulcan on his first space voyage fill the shoes of the legendary Mr. Spock? Xon (pronounced "Zahn") was selected by the Vulcan Science Academy to attempt exactly that. Kirk was stunned when his new science officer reported aboard and found him to be little more than a boy. (Xon looks something like a young Michael York with pointed ears.) Kirk had assumed the replacement was someone near Spock's age. The reports he had read on Xon listed him as a prominent scientist and teacher." Xon was a full Vulcan and a super-genius even by Vulcan standards.

But Xon would be the Science Officer and wouldn't specifically fill Spock's position as executive officer. This position would be held by Commander Will Decker. Although Decker was also the last name of a rogue starship commander in the episode "The Doomsday Machine," this was a fact apparently overlooked by Roddenberry at the time as the characters were not originally intended to be related. By the time Decker appeared in *Star Trek: The Motion Picture*, the relationship was taken as a given.

Lieutenant Ilia was originally spelled "Ilya" until it was pointed out that a male character on *The Man From U.N.C.L.E.* bore the same first name.

The *Star Trek II* writer's guide was essentially an update of the old 1966 *Star Trek* writer's guide. The *Star Trek II* guide in turn had some material transposed into the even more different writers guide for *Star Trek: The Next Generation* ten years later.

In the *Star Trek II* writers guide, Roddenberry wrote, "We will still use science fiction to make comments on today, but today is now a dozen years later than the first Star Trek. Humanity faces many new questions and puzzles which were not obvious back in the 1960s, all of them suggesting new stories and themes. Also, television censorship has relaxed enormously during those same years, opening up still more new story areas, or certainly more honesty in some old areas.

"Television has become much more sophisticated in other ways. Older, ponderous dialogue patterns have given way (thank you, *M.A.S.H.*) to more realism through the use of fragmented sentences, overlaps and interruptions. Better camera techniques, new film emulsions and exciting new optical and tape effects all make increased realism possible.

"*Star Trek* will take more looks into the private and off duty lives of our characters.

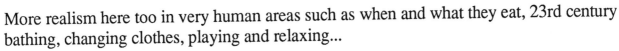

More realism here too in very human areas such as when and what they eat, 23rd century bathing, changing clothes, playing and relaxing...

"The essential format will not change. Action-Adventure entertainment, and some fun for us too as we speculate where we humans are, where we're going and what it's really all about."

Roddenberry also chose this time to exclude the consumption of alcohol from stories, deciding to make Montgomery Scott's love of good scotch the lone exception to the rule. He pointed out that on the sixties *Star Trek* he had resisted pressure to include a 23rd century version of the cigarette, thereby preventing what would have been a big negative on the show come reruns in later years as more and more information about the hazards of smoking became more widely known. He carried this into *The Next Generation* as well by stipulating that all drinks on the Enterprise included a synthetic alcohol which did not inhibit the perceptions of the drinker in any way.

Casting for the new roles continued with David Gautreaux cast as the Vulcan Xon. Persis Khambatta landed the role of Ilia. On October 22, 1977, an article in "The Los Angeles Times" quoted Leonard Nimoy regarding his on-going negotiations with Paramount about his returning as Spock. "I had a good relationship with the Star Trek people. I considered doing the project, but the discussions became very complicated. They went on for a year and a half — it got to the point where I just didn't want to continue with them."

That just stirred up the anger of the fans again, so Roddenberry issued a press release that same day to explain his position and why *Star Trek* would not be crippled by Nimoy's absence. After explaining how much he likes the character of Mr. Spock, and how it became obvious that Leonard Nimoy would not willingly return to the show, Roddenberry stated, "Do we still want Nimoy-Spock in *Star Trek II?* Yes, of course. Must we have the Nimoy-Spock combination back no matter what the schedule or terms or cost? Of course not. We also have obligations on schedule and terms and cost to a Shatner-Kirk combination. And to the other actor-character combinations, too. We have obligations to episode writers who are fine artists in their own right, to a director, to an art director, in fact to well over a hundred other talented actors, staff and crew who are also an important part of *Star Trek*.

"It seems to me that *Star Trek's* content must indicate that I have no small respect for our audience. I must now call upon our audience to return that respect in the form of some confidence that I am trying to make the best *Star Trek II* possible under all the conditions faced in returning the show to television."

And so Roddenberry and company proceeded preparing to get everything ready for filming to begin on November 30, 1977.

But by this time *Star Wars* had gone well past the $100 million mark and was still climbing. The perception of science fiction was changing, particularly with *Close Encounters Of The Third Kind* opening that month. Also, Paramount's fourth network idea had not been as opening embraced by traditional TV advertisers as the studio had hoped. There were unconfirmed rumors that this had happened because ABC, NBC and CBS had uniformly lowered their rates to lure potential sponsors away from Paramount's fledgling network.

Whatever the combination of factors, on November 11, 1977, Paramount halted production on *Star Trek II*, announcing that *Star Trek* would become a motion picture to begin production in 1978. This happened so suddenly that people hired on a Monday, were laid off on Friday the same week.

Although production on *Star Trek II* was halted, key creative people remained to rework set designs, props, etc. for use in a wide-screen motion picture. Harold Livingston remained in his office, reworking the two hour premiere episode script "In Thy Image" into an even more elaborate motion picture script.

While Susan Sackett's 1979 book *The Making Of Star Trek : The Motion Picture* portrays a seamless juxtaposition of the two events, such was not exactly the case. On January 6, 1978, Roddenberry issued a press release to update fans, fan clubs, etc., on the progress of bringing back *Star Trek*. After recapping all that had gone before, he explained, "In October, the Studio became concerned that a made-for-television *Star Trek* was bound to suffer in a comparison with the big-budget *Star Wars* and *Close Encounters*. Paramount decided to commit the Studio's resources to making *Star Trek* a major wide-screen motion picture to be shown in theaters all over the world. Unfortunately, rumors circulated that *Star Trek* was merely being shelved again. This time the rumors were wrong. Production was merely being delayed for the months necessary to let us make *Star Trek* a top quality film event.

"And so this is the situation as of the writing of this letter. We are awaiting the studio's final `go-ahead.' Since the Studio has already invested several million dollars, it looks like it will finally happen this time. On stage, first class *Star Trek* sets, costumes and paraphernalia are ready for the motion picture, and will be standing there — beautiful and ready — for still further *Star Trek* production. Will we make all your efforts and postage stamps and aggravation worthwhile? We can only promise that we will try."

It was shortly thereafter that Paramount gave the final green light necessary to produce a large scale motion picture, then budgeted at $8 to $10 million, which was about what *Star Wars* cost to produce.

From behind-the-scenes, rumors filtered out that Paramount wanted to do a movie but cast it with big-name stars. While this never came close to happening, it was suggested. Said Roddenberry, "They started off wanting to blithely recast. And until six months before we actually began shooting, they were still trying to get Kirk killed off in the first act. `At the very least, Gene, you can promote him to Admiral and bring in a new star,' they said. I refused to do this because I think he [Shatner] is an extraordinarily fine actor."

Never publicly discussed, but as important as the most crucial events was the casting of Leonard Nimoy. He was literally signed only a week before the huge March 28, 1978 press conference held at Paramount Studios, the largest press event the studio had held in twenty years. Although not revealed until *Star Trek : The Motion Picture* opened in December 1979, Nimoy had agreed to make the picture in return for a lump sum settlement of his long standing grievance over non-payment of royalties for the use of his likeness on *Star Trek* products. The fee paid, including his payment for appearing in the motion picture, was reportedly $2.5 million. Paramount had caved into Nimoy's demands due to their belief that a *Star Trek* motion picture could be hurt substantially at the boxoffice without the presence of the one and only Spock.

Once Paramount decided to go for a big budget motion picture, they went all the way. The press event announcing the movie and the acquisition of the entire original cast was just one such example. The biggest press conference held at Paramount since Cecil B. DeMille had announced that he'd be making *The Ten Commandments*, the entire original cast of *Star Trek* was assembled on one stage for the first time since 1969. Also present were Gene Roddenberry and director Robert Wise, who had been signed on some weeks before.

The budget of *Star Trek : The Motion Picture* (the new official name of the project) was now an announced $15 million. The comparisons to *The Ten Commandments* don't just stop at the size of the press conference as that earlier film was made in 1956 for the then unheard of sum of $10 million, the most expensive film of its time. Little did Paramount realize in 1978 that *Star Trek : The Motion Picture* would become the most expensive film of its day by the time of its release Dec. 7, 1979.

At the press conference, the actors appeared on stage in front of a huge backdrop of the newly redesigned Enterprise. While Nimoy was at first reluctant to be serious in the midst of all the hoopla and celebration, a deflected questions about his late signing on the project by saying it takes mail a long time to reach Vulcan.

Star Trek : The Motion Picture may have had a name, but it didn't have a script. The two-hour TV script for the episode "In Thy Image" was still being reworked by various hands, including Harold Livingston. This script was inspired by an old GENESIS II story treatment, "Robot's Return," which Roddenberry had written in 1973. The plot had been expanded into a seventeen page story treatment by Alan Dean Foster in August 1977 and it turn was expanded into a script by Gene Roddenberry and Harold Livingston. Even though the final draft screenplay for the motion picture does not bear Roddenberry's name, his ideas are woven all through it as the plot is essentially a fusion of Roddenberry's rejected 1975 screenplay with the ancient NASA aspects of "Robot's Return." And going back to the original plot outline of "Robot's Return" in the GENESIS II series outline, yet another writer's name emerges. This is how Roddenberry's original brief plot outline reads.

"ROBOT'S RETURN" Suggested by Robert Moore Williams' sf story, this concerns the visit to planet Earth of what appears to be a group of Earth astronauts who have somehow survived on a moon of Jupiter since a late 20th Century space expedition there. Actually, the real astronauts are long dead and the visitors to Earth are actually intelligent robots who evolved out of the complex automated equipment of the expedition and now ultimately reproducing themselves in the form of what they remember as the 'god' who gave them life. A map of the solar system has pointed them to Earth as their beginning point and they have come to worship at the holy home of their creators. At first, the humanoid mechanisms are unable to believe that these helpless creatures on Earth have any connection with their creation. Worse, when they ultimately recognize the truth and realize that this shattered, savage place will someday be reaching out into the solar system again, they doubt if they should permit it to happen.

"This is a 'visit from another planet' story with a strange problem and twist in which these human-looking but mechanical 'children of Man' have developed a power and intelligence which threatens the bond and relationship between them. Wolfe would have agreed that, whether Man or robot, you can't ever go home again."

Roddenberry did an expanded version of this thumbnail plot sketch when GENESIS II was slated to be a CBS series. Roddenberry's expanded and more developed version of this idea changed it considerably, adding elements which seem familiar to us now.

In his story treatment for "Robot's Return," Dylan Hunt hears about the appearance of fantastic machines in a small village. Upon investigating they find that all of the people and animal life in the area of a farm commune have disappeared, the only clue being a small metallic obelisk bearing the symbol of NASA. A strange radio signal is detected in the area which is translated and revealed to be asking, "Wherefore art thou, our God?" Dylan replies on the old radio frequency and a device called The Finder suddenly appears before them in a flash of light, hovering in the air.

When Dylan Hunt tries to identify himself, mentioning his original affiliation with NASA in the 20th century, The Finder demands to know what Dylan knows of God, as its mission is to find NASA, which it has traced to this planet. When three of the PAX team try to flee, The Finder transports them to its vessel in orbit above the Earth. Dylan offers to trade documents he has on NASA for the safe return of his friends. One is returned, and she explains that she was held in a ship which is twenty miles across and contains many life form samples from Earth. Upon checking the records in PAX, they find a cryptic reference to 20th Century expedition to one of the moons of Jupiter where an alien city was found containing functioning machinery but no life.

Later when another prisoner, the woman Harper-Smythe, is beamed down, it becomes apparent that she is a robot probe, a synthetic duplicate of the real Harper-Smythe. They manage to form a liaison with the probe by awakening the human emotions in it as its duplication of Harper-Smythe also included the capability for feeling emotions. The Probe determines that it wants to remain with Dylan and PAX, but Dylan won't jeopardize the captured humans (which are on the ship, waiting to be absorbed as life specimens). After Dylan transmits all his information on NASA to The Finder, the Harper-Smythe robot disappears, leaving the real Harper-Smythe in its place, along with all of the other captured humans. Satisfied that it has learned the truth about NASA, the huge orbiting spacecraft leaves Earth orbit to return to its home world.

The story elements recycled from this are obvious and exist because Alan Dean Foster was given this plot synopsis on which to base his story treatment for the STAR TREK II episode "In Thy Image." Foster's story synopsis reworked the material from "Robot's Return" into the basic concept which was built upon to become *Star Trek : The Motion Picture*. At that time, Alan Dean Foster was best known to Star Trek fans from the writer's successful adaptation and expansion of scripts from the *Star Trek* animated series into the best-selling *Star Trek Log* books. Foster had also ghost written the novelization of the movie *Star Wars* for George Lucas. For reasons which seem obscure now, Foster was not allowed to admit to that fact at the time. Now this is common knowledge even though reprints of the book still maintain only the name of George Lucas as the author of the novel. By 1992, Foster had continued writing science fiction and was the author of 65 books, including 25 TV and movie novelizations.

In Foster's story treatment, a gigantic object is detected in space that is 30 by 70 kilometers in size, and is on a direct course for Earth. The Enterprise approaches it and a signal informs them that it is looking for the god N'sa (pronounced Ensah). Nothing in the Enterprise logs can connect the name of the god to any known cultures in Federation space. The object (which calls itself The Wan) is on its way to Earth because, "N'sa showed the chosen people, 'we the Wan,' the existence and magnificence of the universe. In return, 'we of Wan' wish to return this gift by clearing N'sa's world of the festering disease N'sa indicated was poisoning its surface." Kirk tries to escape from the huge vessel, but the tractor beam holding the Enterprise is too strong. He tries to self-destruct the Enterprise to keep its information from falling into their enemy's hands, but the ship's computer has already been taken over by the alien vessel. The alien vessel intends to clean the Enterprise of the infestations aboard her and probes them for weaknesses by sending various kinds of terrestrial animals aboard (including a swarm of bees) which all turn out to be mechanical devices. When they attempt to communicate with the ship's crew, Kirk is amazed to discover that the ship itself is a single mechanical entity. When Kirk, Xon, Decker and McCoy are allowed to beam aboard the ship, they discover that the old Pioneer 10 spacecraft is aboard. The Wan had accepted the probe as some sort of a manifestation of a god — the god NASA. Kirk proves that humans created the probe and the Wan reluctantly admit that Kirk has proven that humans are a superior intelligent life form. The Enterprise and the Wan go their separate ways.

When it was decided that "In Thy Image" would be the two hour premiere of *Star Trek II*, the TV series, Harold Livingston worked at turning it into a screenplay which he completed October 20, 1977. He added further elements to the story which brought it even closer to what *Star Trek : The Motion Picture* would be.

Livingston's story opens with three Klingon ships encountering an energy force which destroys them. Their destruction is detected by Starbase 9. On Earth, in a San Francisco park, children are playing with animals such as antlered deer and cheetahs which were formerly considered wild. Kirk walks up to a man who is bandaging the paw of the child's pet cheetah. Kirk remarks, "Those cheetahs never pay their bills, Doctor." The doctor in McCoy, who's become a veterinarian as he's embittered by those people he couldn't save during his five year mission on the Enterprise. When Kirk offers McCoy his old position on the newly refurbish Enterprise, the Doctor turns him down flat.

Nogura convinces Kirk to take the Enterprise immediately due to the mysterious alien vessel which is 8.6 days from Earth and no other vessel equipped to deal with a menace of this size is anywhere close enough. The Aswan, a light cruiser, only has half the weapons capabilities of the Klingon ships which were destroyed.

Kirk beams up to the orbiting space dock and he and Scotty use a space pod to travel to the Enterprise due to the fact that the ship's transporters aren't operational yet. Will Decker is aboard, having been abruptly transferred from command of the USS Boston to serve under Kirk on the Enterprise, a fact which Will is bitter about.

When Kirk goes down to the transporter room, Dr. McCoy is beamed aboard, where he reveals that the Federation drafted him back into service much against his will. Lt. Xon is on board as Science Officer. The Enterprise leaves Earth orbit and enters warp drive, where they encounter an asteroid which had been pulled into the path of the starship. Photon torpedoes destroy the asteroid just in time.

When the Enterprise is preparing to rendezvous with the Aswan, they arrive in time only to see the other starship enveloped by the same energy which absorbed the Klingon ships. They arrive where the alien vessel is and find that it is massive and shaped like an open-ended mountain of metal. The Enterprise launches a probe, but it's instantly destroyed by the alien vessel. The ship is suddenly gripped by a tractor beam which the Enterprise cannot break free of as the vessel continues heading towards Earth.

Xon explains that he's discovered that the alien had sent a message to the Enterprise at one million megahertz which revealed that the alien considers the Enterprise itself to be a lifeform. The alien had been communicating directly with the ship's computer until Xon broke contact, but he believes that the alien already secured vital information on the ship through this contact.

Probes of light appear on the Enterprise and begin exploring it, but when they attempt to link up with the computer, Chekov uses his phaser on them, destroying all but one, which disappears on its own, presumably to report back to the alien vessel. When the lone probe returns, it demands to speak directly to USS Enterprise, but Kirk refuses, stating that he is in command. The probe refuses to accept this concept of humans controlling a machine. When he asks the probe why the alien vessel is headed towards Earth, it explains that the planet is the Holy Home of the Creator.

When the Probe contacts the computer against his wishes, Xon smashes the control panel and stops the linkage, but his hands are burned in the process. When Ilia attempts to go to his aid, she and the Probe are enveloped in turquoise light and vanish from the bridge of the Enterprise.

Kirk is resting in his quarters when a burst of light awakens him and Lt. Ilia appears nude in his sonar shower. He covers her with a robe. He quickly realizes that this is not Ilia, but rather a robotic duplicate. The Ilia Probe explains that she has been sent by "Vejur" to learn why the humans infest Enterprise and their importance in relation to it.

The Ilia Probe explains that Vejur wishes to meet with them and so Kirk and Xon transport with her over to Vejur, which has released the Enterprise from the tractor beam as a show of good faith. Ilia leads them to the heart of Vejur where they find an old Voyager 18 space probe which disappeared into a black hole near the end of the 1990's. When Kirk tries to explain that the humans created the Voyager probe, an energy beam knocks Kirk to the floor and Ilia states, "V'ger punishes those who lie."

The Ilia Probe tells Kirk to take the Enterprise on ahead to Earth and to tell the higher life forms (the machines) of V'ger's impending arrival and of the return of the Creator. Kirk tells Uhura to have Starfleet ready all records which prove the existence of NASA and its creation of the Voyager 18 satellite.

Xon is able to get enough information from the Ilia Probe to figure out that Voyager 18 crashed on a planet of machines which considered Voyager their savior, and upon developing space travel capabilities set out to find Voyager 18's homeworld.

The Enterprise reaches Earth several hours ahead of V'ger and Kirk beams down with the Ilia Probe to show her what Earth is really like.

When V'ger arrives in Earth orbit, it launches neutron devices designed to eliminate all life on Earth when they achieve their designated positions. On Earth, Kirk and Ilia visit a beach and then go to the Starfleet Archives building. The Ilia Probe is shown films about the history of NASA and Voyager, but she dismisses them as being just simulations. But on the other hand this duplicate of Ilia seems to be developing human feelings for Kirk as

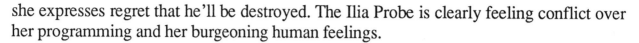

she expresses regret that he'll be destroyed. The Ilia Probe is clearly feeling conflict over her programming and her burgeoning human feelings.

When the designated time of destruction arrives, nothing happens. Ilia explains that she told V'ger that the human servo units are indeed what conceived what they called The Creator. Thus V'ger recognizes the value of humanity and allows them to live.

Back on the Enterprise the real Ilia is returned and the Probe goes inert. Kirk can only believe that this is what the Probe wanted, to cease to exist in this way.

Kirk informs the crew that this successful mission was the shakedown cruise of the renovated Enterprise. "Is that what it was?" McCoy laughs. When the crew is offered the opportunity to beam down to Earth, no one expresses the desire to do so, and so the Enterprise returns to space on the mission it was created for.

While this script by Harold Livingston is what was intended for the two-hour premiere of *Star Trek II*, it is substantially similar to what became *Star Trek : The Motion Picture*. One of the most surprising features of this story is that Spock's absence doesn't harm the story in the slightest. Reading through it we see instead that the story was so far along that by the time Leonard Nimoy signed on to rejoin the cast, the script had to be altered to accommodate him, but those alterations did not significantly affect the story. Rather all of Spock's scenes can now be viewed as filler and add-ons, some of which Roddenberry lifted intact from his 1975 *Star Trek* screenplay, most notably Spock's meeting on Vulcan with the Vulcan masters before he returns to the Enterprise.

There are other things interesting about this story as well. The scene in the park in San Francisco when Kirk meets McCoy is actually much more effective than the filmed version. It establishes some background to the characters so that McCoy's reluctance to rejoin the Enterprise is better explicated.

The problems with the story are the same problems with the movie. The Enterprise is the only starship close enough to Earth to protect it? This is about as likely as it would be for any major alien world not having starships close by to protect it. Surely something more imaginative than this could have been devised for explaining why the Enterprise is the best ship for the job.

Androids developing human emotions is an idea on *Star Trek* as old as the V'ger concept, which was way too similar to the episode "The Changeling" from the sixties series second season, where an Earth space probe collided with an alien probe to create a fusion of the two into something new and different. While the familiar ground may have made it seem like the old *Star Trek*, it also robbed the story of its freshness and surprise.

While *Star Trek : The Motion Picture* was criticized for its virtual worship of special visual effects, elements of that already existed in Harold Livingston's script in the form of the space pod traveling around the renovated Enterprise when Kirk beams up to the space dock to inspect the ship.

The character of Xon is basically a typical Vulcan in this and doesn't have much of a personality to interact with yet. Decker, on the other hand, is resentful of Kirk for yanking him from command of his own starship, the Boston, to serve as first officer on the Enterprise. In the movie this is altered to have Decker replaced as Captain of the Enterprise by Kirk, although whatever personality conflicts this would have resulted in were lost in the rewrites on the movie as Decker pretty much accepts the demotion with all the annoyance one would express while having just a bad day rather than an interrupted career.

After Alan Dean Foster had turned in his treatment of "In Thy Image," and before Harold Livingston turned it into a script, Gene Roddenberry wrote a 98 page expanded treatment which Harold Livingston worked from in writing his script for the TV series and which continued to serve as inspiration through subsequent rewrites of the script as it was transformed into a motion picture. Roddenberry also used material from this when writing his novelization of the movie script which contains material not found in any actual drafts of the screenplays. The following is an overview of material from this 98 page treatment and focuses on the differences between it and Livingston's screenplay of "In Thy Image."

The story opens with Kirk on Earth, swimming in the Pacific Ocean with his lover, Alexandria Keys. (She would be renamed Lori Ciani in the novel.)

Kirk's wrist communicator summons him to Admiral Nogura's office at Starfleet Command, and while traveling there with Alexandria the splendors of 23rd Century Earth are unveiled.

Nogura reveals what happened to the Klingon ships and that the alien intruder is on a course for Earth. He asks Kirk to take command of the Enterprise.

"Jim," Nogura asks, "I haven't asked your feelings on this; I haven't the option of even considering them. Are there any personal obligations we can help you with?"

"No, sir," Kirk replies. "There was someone who I'd decided to discuss a marriage contract with, but it will have to wait until I'm back."

Outside the office Kirk explains to Alexandria that he has no choice and asks her to extend apologies and explanations all around. [In the motion picture, we never see what happens in Nogura's office and in fact are left with the impression that it was Kirk's idea to resume command of the Enterprise, not the other way around. The novel puts it in these terms as well.

Also, Kirk has no girlfriend in the film. In the novel it explains that Lori Ciani was working for Starfleet to keep Kirk on the path Starfleet chose for him and Kirk had only just discovered that.

After Kirk is on board the Enterprise, he goes to the transporter room to meet his Vulcan science officer, Ronak, who is about to beam up. But as two people are beaming aboard, there is a transporter malfunction and the two die. Kirk is shocked to learn that the woman who died is Alexandria, who had volunteered for duty at the last minute in order to be with Kirk. [In the novel, Kirk no longer loves the woman when she's killed. In the treatment he had planned to marry her and is deeply shocked by her loss.]

The transporter is repaired and Xon beams aboard, followed by McCoy, who was drafted back into service. Kirk forces himself to deal with the loss of the woman he loves while preparing to leave Earth orbit.

The asteroid incident in warp drive occurs just as it does in Harold Livingston's script. Also the Aswan is destroyed and the Enterprise is captured in the tractor beam just as it is in Livingston's script. Remember that Livingston's script was actually based more on this expansion of Alan Dean Foster's shorter treatment, even though Livingston's name alone appears on the script. Everything else is the same until the Enterprise returns to Earth ahead of V'ger to prepare for its coming.

On Earth, Lt. Xon develops the hypothesis that it might be possible to beam the pattern of a human brain into the main circuitry of V'ger which would allow the intelligence of an organic life form to link with the computer mind for a more complete understanding. Decker is beamed into V'ger and joins with it, becoming one, each sharing the thoughts of the other. An understanding is reached and the neutron devices orbiting Earth are deactivated. Decker states through the computer that perhaps one day V'ger can return him to human form as the transporter has a record of his full physical pattern. V'ger disappears from orbit and vanishes into space. The Ilia Probe goes inert and the real Ilia is returned to the Enterprise.

Although this version of the ending was not incorporated by Harold Livingston into the TV script "In Thy Image," certainly a version of it is what became the climax of *Star Trek : The Motion Picture*. Interestingly, when filming on the movie began in the summer of 1978, the conclusion of the script had not yet been worked out even though Roddenberry already had it down on paper nearly a year before in his expanded treatment of "In Thy Image."Once again, this is why even though Roddenberry's name does not appear on the screenplay, his ideas invest the story from beginning to end. In fact, it's surprising that he didn't request credit since documentation of his in-depth contributions to the script would have been easy for him to produce as the Alan Dean Foster treatment was based on a Roddenberry outline and the Harold Livingston "In Thy Image" was based on Roddenberry's 98 page treatment of Foster's story treatment of Roddenberry's story. It seems that barely 50% of the screenplay to *Star Trek: The Motion Picture* can truly be traced to original material added by Livingston at all. That Roddenberry believed this to be true as well is evidenced by the fact that he took the script to credit arbitration five times before the Writer's Guild to attempt to get his name in the final film credits as one

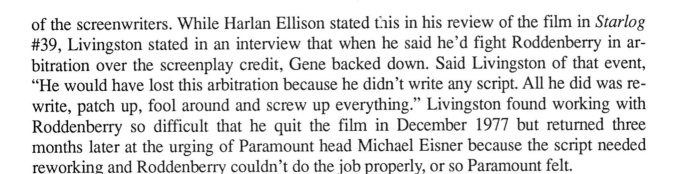

of the screenwriters. While Harlan Ellison stated this in his review of the film in *Starlog* #39, Livingston stated in an interview that when he said he'd fight Roddenberry in arbitration over the screenplay credit, Gene backed down. Said Livingston of that event, "He would have lost this arbitration because he didn't write any script. All he did was rewrite, patch up, fool around and screw up everything." Livingston found working with Roddenberry so difficult that he quit the film in December 1977 but returned three months later at the urging of Paramount head Michael Eisner because the script needed reworking and Roddenberry couldn't do the job properly, or so Paramount felt.

In spite of how similar the final script was to story outlines which had gone before, there was constant work being done rewriting the screenplay from March 1978 even through filming itself. One writer who briefly worked on the script doing a rewrite was Dennis Lynton Clark. Although Clark is described on page 64 of Susan Sackett's *The Making Of Star Trek The Motion Picture* in the capacity of writer, strangely he is never mentioned by name. What is mentioned in the book is a practical joke pulled on Clark involving telling him that Paramount had fired his secretary and replaced her with someone else, who was Grace Lee Whitney in disguise. The problem with this gag was that Clark's secretary/assistant had been with him for years and the thought that Paramount would fire her without consulting him sent Clark into a rage. When he found out it was a joke, he got into a screaming argument with Gene Roddenberry over it because he considered it to be in extremely bad taste. He and Roddenberry never got along well after that and Clark was gone within three months.

Associate producer Jon Povill provided a great deal of input and story meetings were also had involving Robert Wise, William Shatner and Leonard Nimoy. When filming began in the summer of 1978, scenes being shot that day were being rewritten so that the revised script pages sometimes had to list the hour of the revision to insure that the most current one was being used. Livingston, who was supposed to be doing the rewrites, found himself delivering pages to Robert Wise only to find that Roddenberry was rewriting the same pages on the same day in the hope that Wise would like Roddenberry's rewrites better. Listing the hour on the page of the rewrite was done by Roddenberry to make his rewrite look more current than Livingston's, even though Roddenberry wasn't supposed to be doing the rewrites. In fact when Livingston returned to the film, he did so with the express promise from Roddenberry that he wouldn't do any further writing on the script, a promise that Gene quickly broke.

Walter Koenig described the film's story problems in an interview in *Questar* #6. "The trouble really came in the film's third act. That one act went through some fifty or sixty different changes while we were shooting it! We went through six, seven, eight changes a day — they'd be handing us new pages every hour! Then, it wasn't bad enough that Gene, Harold and Bob were fighting over the scripts — after five weeks, Bill and Leonard finally got script approval." But Koenig still felt positive about the final result, at least at that time. "Things did become even more complicated after the fifth week, but when it was all over, I think things pulled together nicely."

In the September 1979 issue of *Fantastic Films*, Robert Wise described the situation that faced him when he signed on to direct the movie. "I came into a situation that was already set in many areas. That's very unusual for me. I'd never worked this way before, and it was kind of a strange feeling. I'm learning to deal with it, finding ways in which I can alter things that have already been set. Since I couldn't start from scratch I've tried to upgrade things and improve them so they'll all come out looking like they belong in the same film."

Wise stressed that the biggest hurdle he faced was the crush of time to finish the special effects. "That was our major problem. The challenge of doing the effects and getting them up there and dealing with them is no problem for me. The time I have to do them in, that everybody has to do them in, is the problem. But I want to make one point that is very important. There is nothing more important on any film than the foreground, the actors, the story. That's what we worked on like a son-of-a-gun. We had to be sure that the story we put in front of these marvelous photographic effects was going to be worthy of them and hopefully hold its own against the special photographic effects, and not suffer by comparison."

When then Paramount president Michael Eisner announced the *Star Trek* motion picture in March 1978, he stated that the visuals, "will be of extreme importance" and revealed that Robert Abel & Associates had been placed in charge of special optical effects. Abel revealed to *Variety* that two thirds of *Star Trek : The Motion Picture* would involve special effects, opticals and animation. Abel was a prize winning maker of commercials whose use of special effects set the industry standard for innovation. In 1978, his was one of the only companies set up specifically to specialize in the use of special optical effects, although many others would come into being within the next couple of years to handle the increasing demands for optical effects in films. John Dykstra's company, Apogee, existed, but he was involved in another project at the time, as was Douglas Trumbull.

According to an article in *New West* magazine for March 26, 1979, Abel's company, in spite of its reputation for excellence, had also become notorious for lateness and cost overruns, so that major commercial clients were beginning to steer clear of him. When Paramount hired him to produce optical effects for *Star Trek : The Motion Picture*, four million dollars was the estimate Abel gave the studio to produce the effects. Abel had originally budgeted them at $6 million but thought that Paramount would balk at that. Then Abel's initial cost estimate of $4 million was upped to $16 million in December 1978, partially based on the fact that the screenplay was undergoing constant rewrites. There was also the fact that Abel's company had never produced optical effects for a motion picture before, having solely worked on thirty and sixty second commercials. Concerned by this, Paramount decided to split the optical effects responsibilities and hired

Douglas Trumbull, whose feature credits for producing opticals included *2001, Silent Running* and *Close Encounters Of The Third Kind*. This was not the first time that Trumbull had been contacted by Paramount to work on *Star Trek : The Motion Picture*

Months earlier, Paramount had offered Trumbull the job to be in charge of the special effects for ST:TMP, but Trumbull turned them down, having just completed *Close Encounters* and having no desire to tackle a job that big again this soon. Paramount even hinted that Trumbull (who had directed *Silent Running*) might also direct *Star Trek: The Motion Picture,* but that overture was never firm. Trumbull was already working for Paramount through his company Future General which Paramount was funding. Part of his duties included consulting on other Paramount projects, and so Trumbull, and his associate Richard Yuricich, began to serve as a liaison between Paramount and Robert Abel's company by the summer of `78.

Trumbull could see that the project was much bigger than Abel's company could ever handle and so in August of `78 he offered to take over doing the effects. Paramount felt that Abel's company could handle it and turned him down. Trumbull continued to serve as a consultant under a special contract set to run for January through March 1979, but it was during this time that Paramount came back to Trumbull and accepted his offer to be in charge of the effects.

"By the time they realized how much trouble they were in," Trumbull told *Cinefex* in the March 1980 issue, "they would have entertained anybody who could have walked in the door and been able to pull them out of the jam. So we finally struck an arrangement that was mutually beneficial."

Once Trumbull took over, many people were brought in to work on miniatures and effects, including John Dykstra's company, Apogee, as well as many freelance technicians. Trumbull reassembled his entire team from *Close Encounters*, including Greg Jein, who had supervised the building of the Mothership model. The Glencoe facility, a warehouse and office complex in Marina del Rey where opticals for *Close Encounters* had been filmed, served as the same sight for that crew's work on *Star Trek : The Motion Picture.*

Trumbull's involvement even extended to work directly involving the live action photography. "The Spock spacewalk, for example, is a total one hundred percent change from the sequence that was designed, built and photographed under Abel's supervision. Both versions start out the same — the Enterprise is stuck inside V'ger and no one knows what's going on; so Spock commandeers a spacesuit and goes outside to snoop around. In the original, however, when Kirk discovers Spock's out there, he gets in a spacesuit and goes after him — in the process of which he's caught up in a mass of sensor-type organisms and nearly killed. Of course, Spock comes back and saves the day, and the two of them continue on together through several different chambers in the V'ger ship."

Trumbull felt this sequence didn't work at all and wasn't as interesting as what had been originally scripted. Plus he believed that the spacesuit designs were poor. Then there was the fact that the optical effects needed to still be combined with the live action photography would be so extensive that it would require half the special effects budget of the picture to finish the sequence, one which Trumbull felt was dull and slowed the story down to a crawl. "We had a screening of the rough cut, and when it came to the spacewalk the whole movie just fell apart. What they'd done was produce a very literalized and simplistic version of a concept which in the script was really kind of mind boggling. And in spite of the fact that they'd already spent a million dollars on the sequence, it was apparent to me that it was going to cost about half of our total special effects budget and most of our resources just to save it with matte paintings and opticals and make the effects work somewhat as designed. But even at best I never thought it was going to net a very exciting result because the whole concept was just boring.

"So it was my recommendation," Trumbull continued, "to scrap the whole sequence and start over. With all the money and effort they'd already expended, it took a bit of doing to convince everyone that it should be abandoned outright; but once everybody agreed that we should take another shot at it, I sat down and wrote a new spacewalk sequence based on some ideas I wanted to try which I felt we could do in the time we had. Basically, it was my intent to try and find a way to put some of the magic back in and turn it into a dynamic, exciting sequence that would blitz by in two or three minutes and be over with so the story could carry on. I decided not to involve Kirk at all, and just redesign it as a personal thing for Spock — a high-speed psychedelic trip through the stored images and memories of everything V'ger had encountered during its journey."

Pieces of the discarded sequence involving Kirk exist in the current version of *Star Trek : The Motion Picture* available on home video when Kirk dons his spacesuit and exits the Enterprise to retrieve Spock's unconscious body as Kirk's spacesuit which he puts on inside the Enterprise is different from the one he's wearing when he makes contact with Spock. The unfinished nature of that early footage is unfortunately apparent as Kirk descends from an Enterprise which has wooden rafters above him and to his left clearly visible. This is raw footage wherein the visible parts of the soundstage would have been covered with matte paintings had the sequence not been abandoned unfinished. Its inclusion in the home video in this state was an oversight as it would have been left out entirely had the state of the footage been noticed in time by the proper personnel. The scrapped footage of the trench and what was referred to as the memory wall accounted for $380,000 in set construction costs alone which had to be written off. The discarded scenes exist now only as part of Gene Roddenberry's novelization of the film.

The spacesuits originally designed for the film had helmets that looked like the very last word in science fiction for 1949 the helmets looked like Sparkletts water bottles. Regarding the suits themselves, Brick Price stated, "We had originally designed the spacesuit for air conditioning so you wouldn't have a problem with fog on the faceplate, and also for the comfort of the actors. They had these stupid rubber wetsuits and we wanted to use dance:skins. We found some material that would have been wonderful, but they ended up using this pudgy stuff which was real hot and sweaty. At one point I walked into the sound stage into what they called the trench sequence, which they ultimately abandoned. It had awful looking plastic pyramids in it and when I walked around the corner to view the angle of the camera, nobody was there. I thought at first that someone was fooling around because they had a dummy in a suit hanging up there and it looked like someone had been hung. Suddenly I realized and shouted, `Oh My God! You're killing Spock!' They took him down and it turned out that Nimoy had passed out from the carbon dioxide collecting in his suit. The heat had built up and become unbearable. There are wires that came up through the crotch and could strangle you around the waist and it's unbearable inside a wetsuit and helmet."

The new spacewalk sequence with Spock involved Nimoy returning to shoot the new scenes. This was apparently done in July as Roddenberry remarked on August 2nd, 1979 that principal photography had just been completed.

Greg Jein and his crew weren't hired on to build the models for that sequence until a month later, around the 6th of September. "Our involvement originally was just doing the elements for Spock's space walk. For instance, the planets, the inner surfaces, the V'ger moon, V'ger egg, and `lips in space' as we call them. Then about three or four weeks into the production, Doug (Trumbull) called me over to his office and said, `We've got one more miniature to build and its got no real designs on it. It's the interior of V'ger and it's kind of important to the film, so you guys better swing on that.' So we just started working on it using some blueprints by Syd Mead. I had to build a miniature from the drawings so I could visualize how we were going to build it."

Since Greg Jein and his crew didn't start work until three months before the release date of the movie, their schedule was unusually hectic. "Usually on a show," Jein explained, "the company is concerned about the money being spent and the material, labor and things like that. But in this case, Paramount just said, `Do it. Work hundreds of hours a week,' which we did! For a couple weeks we worked a hundred hours a week; sometimes we never left here, just stayed here three days straight. They just wanted it done for the show. As it was progressing it sort of `grew.' More and more lighting was used to make it look better; we wound up using 23 miles of Fibre Optics."

While the impending release date meant that a lot of work had to be done in a short amount of time, Jein explained that Paramount wasn't unpleasant to them in the way they applied pressure to meet their deadlines, but there was pressure nonetheless. "There was always a subtle pressure. There was no one screaming that you were going to get fire, because if you were fired they'd have no one to do it anyway. We had 24-hour crews working here.

"We were constantly being visited by production people from Paramount saying, `Could you do it a little faster? Don't go out for dinner; we'll bring it in to you.' I don't remember exactly, but we were about three days over the deadline, and we were the first ones to get our section done. Other sections came along about a week later. So they were sort of ticked off at us at first, but as things progressed they lightened up on us. It was very close. I'm almost positive we were shooting up to three weeks before the release date."

Even after the optical chores were expanded and farmed out to a number of facilities, the infighting continued. Brick Price Movie Miniatures, who built props for the film, as well as the spacesuit used by Spock (although they received no on-screen credit due to an oversight), found that out when they visited Magicam. "Magicam wanted to do everything with the effects and miniatures themselves, even though they were overloaded and understaffed," Brick Price recalled. "One day we went down there to collaborate on something, because we were all working on the same film. When I got there and was introduced they literally slammed the door in my face! As far as I know, we and all the other groups got along extremely well."

Brice Price wasn't the only one who reported problems working with Magicam. In the March 1980 issue of *Fantastic Films*, Andrew Probert, who designed many of the major models in the film, including the new look of the Enterprise and the Klingon ships, reported an altercation as well.

""Yes, well I did have a rather interesting first encounter with Magicam. When I first visited their shop and saw a partially built Klingon cruiser, it was apparent to me that its neckpiece was crooked, and as part of my newly assigned responsibilities, brought this to their attention. The design of the cruiser, with its varying proportions and angles, was such that no one else had noticed it and when I came out of the blue with my observation it didn't go over too well. They told me, once that it was brought to their attention, that it would cost too much time and money to correct. As it turned out, at a much later time in the production, the need arose for a structural change, so the neck was realigned at that time. But from that time forward, however, nothing in the way of design or drawing submitted by me was ever acceptable to Magicam."

The fact was that even with the shop run by Douglas Trumbull, as well as John Dykstra's studio and others, *Star Trek : The Motion Picture* had companies working seven days a week, and sometimes 24 hours a day in order to produce the needed opticals for what was admittedly a special effects laden film. As it was, the film was finally completed without the participation of Robert Abel's company as he was fired on Feb. 22, 1979. By that time, Paramount's March 1978 budget estimate of $15 million estimate for the film had now doubled to $30 million.

Regarding the much publicized dismissal of Bob Abel's group, Brick Price (whose shop built props for the film), felt that Abel was unfairly maligned in the article done in *New West* magazine, and that as far as he was concerned, "Abel wanted to do a good film. Bob was constantly having battles with Magicam and Paramount and ultimately with Doug Trumbull. Trumbull was working for Paramount and as far as I knew, Bob was working with them and they were moving onward. That business about a minute and a half worth of film being all they (Abel) had is ludicrous because I saw that much the first day of rushes. The first day I started working on the film I saw more than that amount of footage. But the thing was, Paramount would see something they wouldn't like, such as the spacewalk, and want to reshoot."

While none of the final optical effects generated by Robert Abel's company made it into the, some live action special effects Abel's crew shot does appear on screen in the form of the glowing V'ger probe which appears on the bridge. Mike Minor, who worked as an illustrator and sort of an assistant art direction on the film describes how that footage was accomplished.

"A man wore a black suit and walked about doing it. You'll notice that to wipe him out of the shot they had to do a split; a left and right split. You might notice as the thing moves across the curved proportions of the bridge you will see one side of the bridge does not quite match up to its counterpart on the right side of the screen because they were joining two images to wipe the operator out, and to wipe out the device which was a tube six feet tall and about a foot in diameter which had big, powerful florescent tubes inside. That was something they rigged; forty thousand volts on that step generator. They blew the power transformers at Paramount and had to bring in a special truck generator just to run that device. Tremendous amount of voltage; a scary device. That device was shot by them (Bob Abel's company) and the effects material was turned over eventually to either Dykstra or Trumbull."

Minor explained that a lot of live action footage was cut from the film. "For instance, when they did the wing-walk on the hull of the ship, we had blacked out a whole stage and set up the hexagonal cubes that they step off of the ship and walk across to V'ger's brain section. We had originally planned to have the cubes light up. Now you can get scuttled as a designer by your cameraman, and this cameraman, Richard Kline, didn't like the look; was afraid of it. I think his gaffer and he were afraid to try to light it. Cubes were supposed to light up as they walked on them. It could have been a great look. There was a wonderful fluttering glow in all of them. We did a test, it looked fine, but inexplicably they wound up being painted grey so you had this cold, dull look. I had built a number of pieces which hung as `chandelier' units which were revealed by electric bursts within them and then they winked out and you couldn't see them. These were hung out in front of the ship and they were to be on and off as forms that were lit by electrical bursts in the void and then disappear and leave electrical energy about them for a moment, and we did it live. We were rushing to get the thing done and they were built mechanically.

They worked on that stuff for a month with me designing and them executing in Plexiglass, opaque materials, back-lighting them, wiring the thing and L.E.D.'s. I remember them being hung there and Trumbull and I standing there with our arms folded, looking up, and I looked over and said, `Well, do you think they're going to make it into the picture?' and he just shook his head and said, `No.' But they let us go ahead and play with this just the same."

Interestingly, Douglas Trumbull had some complimentary things to say about the way Robert Abel's group conceived the look of the climax of the film. In the March 1980 *Cinefex*, Trumbull stated, "There had been some incredibly elaborate storyboards done at Abel's for this beautiful transformation thing, which was along the lines of a cocoon changing into a butterfly — literally — huge sets of wings folding out and all these other diaphanous things. There were a lot of very nice ideas, but I could never get a handle on exactly how to do it, particularly in the amount of time we had left."

That *Star Trek : The Motion Picture* is a major special effects extravaganza is undeniable, but it didn't start out that way. In an interview with Gene Roddenberry on August 4, 1978, shortly after filming had begun, he stated, "Let me also say, though, that it's still going to be *Star Trek*. We didn't take a look at *Star Wars* or *Close Encounters* and say, 'Oh, wow, we've got to change and be all opticals and that sort of stuff." Maybe Roddenberry didn't make that decision, but somebody did. A year later, On August 3, 1979, Roddenberry had this to say. "Beginning with *Star Wars and Close Encounters* and all that type of thing, the post-production work on SF gets larger and larger because science fiction movies are sort of going the direction of becoming total sensations. Sound is very important and the use of opticals today is often almost an exercise in computer lore. It is enormously more complex than in those that we used to do on early *Star Trek* — punch holes in a black screen with a pin and put a light behind them and say, `Okay, move those and they will be the stars!' It's far from that day."

A gauge of the behind-the-scenes difficulties in making *Star Trek: The Motion Picture* can only partially be found in Susan Sackett's March 1980 book. Proof of this is the fact that the name of Robert Abel appears on only three pages in the book, with basically a year of participation in the project reduced to its barest essentials. While Sackett's book, *The Making Of Star Trek The Motion Picture*, waxes long on the trials of writing the screenplay, the optical effects remain largely offstage and consolidated into chapter twenty alone, as though they were merely a secondary element of the project the way the optical effects in the television series were. Reportedly there were plans for a separate book on the making of the visual effects of *Star Trek : The Motion Picture*, but this never materialized, for reasons I'll discuss later.

Another gauge of the behind-the-scenes problems is the almost complete lack of behind-the-scenes footage. While *Star Wars* had produced enough for a television special with some left over, only about ten minutes have ever been seen on *Star Trek : The Mo-*

tion Picture. This footage shows Abel's people with their light generating device on the bridge (which was later covered by an optical), as well as scenes of Persis Khambatta getting her head shaved, when she burst into tears. It's quite startling to see, although I'm not aware that this has even been shown on television. I saw it at a convention several years ago and I've surprised people by describing it as it was believed that no such footage exists.

While Susan Sackett's book goes on about how good-natured Robert Wise was, tales persist that he was difficult to work with. The behind-the-scenes footage is one example. Little footage of this kind exists because Wise reportedly barred that documentary crew from the set after three days because he felt they got in his way.

Walter Koenig described an early encounter with Robert Wise in an interview in the February 1980 issue of *Questar*. "The junior members were really shuffled over. I felt that each of us has fans numbering in the thousands, but it was `no soap.' I felt that in our first scene there should have at least been a tight shot on George, on Nichelle, and so forth, but no way. There just wasn't time to please everybody. And I can see their point; they had to concentrate on the money players. Bill and Leonard and DeForest had to receive the greatest attention. I tried, but it was awful. On the first day of shooting, I asked director Bob Wise for a close-up for Chekov, and I still shudder to think of his answer. He looked at me and said,` Don't ask me such an actorish thing.' I suffered over that."

Roddenberry himself later attributed the problems in the film to the fact that in television the producer controls the show, whereas in movies the director has the last word.

Also, part of the reason that Nimoy reportedly wanted to kill off Spock in *Star Trek II: The Wrath Of Khan* was because his experience making *Star Trek : The Motion Picture* was not a pleasant one and it was because Nimoy enjoyed working with director Nicholas Meyer so much on *The Wrath of Khan* that he started having second thoughts about killing off Spock.

The size of this production was evidenced by the fact that eleven of Paramount's thirty-two sound stages were used during filming, and four of them were used twice.

The largest single set was the rec room where Kirk delivers his speech to some of the starship crew about what they're going to be up against. Most of the 170 men and 20 women in this scene were recruited from *Star Trek* fandom rather than from the regular pool of screen extras who normally try out for such roles. An audition was held for these roles on October 9, 1978 at Paramount Studios and the only real requirements were that they be between the ages of 20 and 40 and that the men range in height from 5'8" to 6'2" and the women be from 5'6" to 5'8" in order to fit into the existing uniforms already made for this scene. A few of the fans chosen were made up to be aliens, including some female Vulcans. The reason that fans were chosen to be in this scene was Gene Roddenberry's way of saying thank you to at least some of the fans whose diligent support had helped bring *Star Trek* back from the land of cancellation. The actual rec room scene was shot about a week after the costume fittings were done.

Not all of those who appeared in that scene were fans as some were members of the Screen Extras Guild. Waivers had been obtained from the Guild to allow the 190 fans to participate as a total of some 300 people actually crowded into the Rec Room set in order to attempt to show virtually the entire crew of the Enterprise in one scene. There weren't 430 people there though, aside from the fact that everyone couldn't be there or who would be on duty elsewhere in the ship?

The fact that non-members of the Screen Extras Guild were participating (and being paid about $75.00 a day for their time there), irked some Guild members, who took the opportunity to pass out literature denouncing the use of waivers in any motion picture. What they expected to accomplish by passing these protests out to the people who benefited from the waivers remains obscure. Some Guild members may have felt picked on because the Screen Extras Guild has had an uphill fight getting respect and recognition over the years, as members of the Screen Actors Guild long opposed having the two guilds merge as they considered extras to be unskilled performers since they can't speak any dialogue in a film (unless they also belong to the Screen Actor's Guild) and basically just walk or sit around in scenes in order to provide background and atmosphere.

Among the many fans who appeared on screen (and don't blink or you'll miss them) are David Gerrold, Bjo Trimble and Kathleen Sky as well as many others who, thirteen years later, may not even be fans of the series any more!

This scene is marred by poor directing in that the two story set has large ports near the top through which a huge painted cyclorama of the nacelles of the Enterprise can be scene — except for the fact that Robert Wise had people stand in front of these ports obscuring the $30,000 cyclorama. Having these people stand up there clutters up the scene whereas if they weren't blocking the windows the scene would have had a sense of depth and dimension to it which is otherwise missing.

Basically what the people in the rec room scene did was stand at attention and look at a blank screen while Robert Wise told them what they were reacting to. "Now you see the enemy strike again," the director explained. "It's awesome. You're horrified! You can't believe it! React!" While two days had been scheduled to shoot this scene, Wise managed to get all the shots he needed in one day by going into overtime hours. Although photos were shot of this scene by the film's still photographer, the only ones I've ever scene published appeared in *Starlog* #20 and #40. None appeared in Susan Sackett's book, nor was mention made of the involvement of fans in the rec room scene even though Sackett herself appeared in the scene. This may have been cut due to the problems with some Screen Extra Guild members and the decision not to officially issue information on a situation which could reopen old wounds. The result is that the description of the logistics involved in filming the rec room scene remains conspicuous by its absence.

On screen in the film during the rec room scene is the sequence in which the Epsilon 9 space station relays their contact with V'ger. The young Starfleet officer on the screen is David Gautreaux, the young actor who had been cast in 1977 as Xon in the never filmed STAR TREK II television series. In *Starlog* #136, Gautreaux explained why he did not play Xon in the motion picture and why the character was written out entirely.

"I was doing a play at the time," Gautreaux recalls, "trying not to think that I was going to be playing an alien for the rest of my life. Then, I spoke to Gene Roddenberry and said, `What's the story? Did you see that Leonard Nimoy is coming back to play his character? What's going to happen to Xon?' He said, `Oh, Xon is very much a part of the family and you're very much a part of our family.' I responded, `Gene, don't allow a character of this magnitude to simply carry Spock's suitcases on board the ship and then say, I'll be in my quarters if anybody needs me. Give him what I've put into him and what you've put into him. If he's not going to be more a part of it and more noble than that, let's eliminate him.' And that's what we did."

Security on the sets of the film was tight, partially because some items had been stolen early in the production. One of the stolen items were blueprints for the sets which someone had copied and was selling to diehard fans even though the blueprints in question were never actually used on the film, having been discarded and replaced with a different design. People had to wear special security badges to get on the set Even Walter Koenig was barred entry at one point when he brought his family down to visit the sets on the day when the rec room scene was being filmed. Other than the question of theft by zealous fans, what they had to hide is questionable because copies of the script to the film were being sold months before the movie's release. This is not unusual. In fact, in the last ten years the only script I've heard of which was not obtainable on the black market prior to the film's was TERMINATOR 2. When Oliver Stone was directing JFK he had to fend off questions about the film from reporters who had already read a draft of the film as the script had already gotten out. The reason it's so rare when this doesn't happen is because dozens of copies of a script exist during production for not just the actors, but for special effects people as well so they can see the context in which an effect is used. So months before the film's release, fans were already upset over the similarity of the story to previous *Star Trek* television episodes.

Roddenberry addressed this issue in the November 1980 issue of *Starlog*. "After having done 78 [sic] episodes covering a fairly wide field, it would have been hard to do anything and not have it bear some resemblances. I think that [the film] appeared to resemble [certain episodes] more at the end because many of the things that made the script different were, bit by bit, sliced out of the movie. They were the `talky' things. The personal stories were excised from the script or the shooting schedule. Then it became...more and more like things we had done in the past." Roddenberry traced these problems back to the fact that, "we had a two-hour television script, which that story was right for, rather than being given the time to...really get the major motion picture story. Had we done that, we probably would've had none of those complaints and an even better film."

When *Star Trek : The Motion Picture* was released on Dec. 7, 1979, it received mixed reviews from both the media and the fans. While there were long lines at the boxoffice and it grossed over $100 million, many were disappointed, including director Robert Wise. At the Washington, D.C. premiere, Wise was seen to cover his face during some scenes as he'd requested more time to edit and fine tune the film, but Paramount said there wasn't any time left. December was upon them. It's release length of 132 minutes seemed even longer as the picture was not only talky, but the special optical effects were treated with undue reverence, as though the audience was expected to stare at them in awe. It also has a peculiarly sterile quality which isn't entirely the result of the pale costumes. Robert Wise reportedly felt that the TV show costumes looked like pajamas, but the ones used in his film looked even more like pajamas! Nicholas Meyer discarded them entirely for the second film with the proclamation, "There will be no Doctor Dentons on my bridge!"

A re-edited version of the film premiered on ABC a couple years later and was actually much improved. Character scenes and telling lines of dialogue were added, and even though it swelled the running time to 143 minutes, the film played much better. This is the version currently available on home video. The pacing still drags, but it's interesting to view in light of the five sequels as it has a style uniquely its own, one which aimed at spectacle of the kind only achievable on the wide screen. It is most successful at this during Spock's voyage through V'ger. The sickbay scene, when Spock confronts his human side and describes his feelings to Kirk, still has a lot of snap to it and one wishes that the rest of the writing in the picture was as strong as this. Roddenberry's novelization indicates further story possibilities that the film had, if only they had been followed through with instead of the long, lingering stare sessions with optical effects.

It is this very problem which was confronted in the opening paragraph of Richard Schickel's TIME magazine review of the film in the December 17, 1979 issue. In a review titled "Warp Speed to Nowhere," Schickel wrote, "It used to be that special effects were created to serve a movie's story, to permit the camera to capture that which could not be found — or recorded on film — in the natural world. But now, in the post-*Star Wars* era, stories are created merely to provide a feeble excuse for the effects. *Star Trek* consists almost entirely of this kind of material: shot after shot of vehicles sailing through the firmament to the tune of music intended to awe. But the spaceships take an unconscionable amount of time to get anywhere, and nothing of dramatic or human interest happens along the way."

In the issue of *Newsweek* for the same date, reviewer Jack Kroll stated, "Producer Gene Roddenberry, who created the TV series, and veteran director Robert Wise are trapped between media. They want to keep the rhythm and intimacy of the TV show while latching on to the epic advantages of the movie format. But in making this maneuver, they fall on their asteroids. The deliberate pace that can be perversely hypnotic on TV expands to a large soporific cloud on the giant screen. And despite the efforts of special effects magicians Douglas Trumbull and John Dykstra, *Star Trek* never gives your mind the push provided by a Kubrick, a Lucas or a Spielberg at his best."

The evidence that *Star Trek*: *The Motion Picture* wasn't exciting audiences to the degree expected was evident on the marketing end. Numerous toys, books and other material related to the movie had been licensed but sales on them were sluggish. Susan Sackett's book *The Making Of Star Trek : The Motion Picture* was by no means a best-seller and today remains a difficult item to come by. Even more difficult to find is the hardcover book club edition I acquired at the time.

Due to the slow sales of that title and of Walter Koenig's personal diary of his experiences on the film, *Chekov's Enterprise*, plans for a book entirely on the making of the special visual effects of the film were abruptly cancelled. That an odor of failure lingered with the *Star Trek* film was still evident when *Star Trek II: The Wrath Of Khan* was released in June 1982 with very few tie-in products connected to it.

There wasn't even a comic book adaptation of the film even though Marvel Comics had done a magazine format adaptation of *Star Trek : The Motion Picture*. (This Marvel adaptation had its own troubled history as an article on the TV series done as a back-up feature in the magazine was ordered altered by Paramount to remove all photos taken from the sixties series as they didn't want the cheaply made TV show tied in with their expensive motion picture, which makes as little sense today as it did then.)

Paramount was clearly looking for a hit on the order of *Star Wars and Close Encounters,* but fell somewhat short of their goal. While a $100 million box office is clearly no small feat, when stacked up against a motion picture with a troubled history and massive cost overruns which elevated the production costs above the $40 million range, something on a higher order was expected to offset these problems. When the picture didn't deliver all that Paramount expected of it, they went looking for someone to blame, and that someone was the producer of the film: Gene Roddenberry.

It took several months for the studio to do this though as the film played many venues for several months. In 1979 home video and cable weren't the massive parts of the marketplace they are today, and even as late as 1982 films like E.T. continued to play theaters for as long as a year. So in early 1980, while Paramount was eyeing the performance of *Star Trek : The Motion Picture* with a critical eye, Roddenberry continued to work in his office at the studio and even wrote a sequel script and turned it in. But in July 1980 the studio asked Roddenberry and his secretary, Susan Sackett, to pack up and leave the Paramount lot. Any plans for a sequel motion picture had been shelved for at least a year.

Even before Paramount made it clear that they weren't as happy with Roddenberry in 1980 as they were in 1979, the creator of *Star Trek* was expressing his annoyance at the barbs both fans and critics alike had been hurling at his movie. In the November 1980 issue of *Starlog* (#40), he discussed his feelings in an interview done with Karen E. Willson shortly before Roddenberry was asked to move off the Paramount Studios lot.

"I was surprised to see some of the top critics make the assumption that [making the film] was as simple as: You take this television thing and you put it on a larger screen and therefore you've made a motion picture. This is the first time a television show ever became a major motion picture, and Robert Wise did a remarkable job in adapting from one medium to another. Many people don't seem to be aware that they're two entirely different mediums.

"Major motion picture spectacle doesn't lend itself easily to Mr. Spock's cute little remarks with Captain Kirk," Roddenberry continued. "The conversion of a two-hour television show into a movie was much more difficult than anyone could've believed. And we just kept not getting what Robert Wise needed to make it into a movie...it wasn't because anyone was delinquent or anyone didn't think to have..." Roddenberry stops a moment, visibly angered. "Y'know, they sometimes say that as if we didn't think to have a script ready and on hand. We worked our bleeping tails off! And kept throwing away much of what we did.

"Some of the [critics'] attitudes are simply not well reasoned out. Critics have been bemoaning for many years the amount of violence on TV and in the movies, saying that two people shooting at each other is not drama...then they proceed to ignore the fact that in *St:Tmp* there was little or no violence at all. But **Star Wars**, which they praise as the definitive science fiction film, has it. I liked *Star Wars* [he saw it four times]; it was fun. But there's no continuity in the critic's demands and criticisms." Which is not entirely true, as there's a difference between criticizing gratuitous violence and genuine dramatic conflict which arises out of legitimate story concerns. But Roddenberry never defended *Star Trek : The Motion Picture* uncritically himself.

"My attitude on *Star Trek* is this." Roddenberry stated. "I think that while the film failed in a number of areas where I would have liked it to have succeeded, it was a successful adaptation of the television story to the screen. We could have done more — and we could have done a lot less, but we did what we could under the time, conditions and circumstances — and the fact that God double-crossed us by making us fallible. The film has some failures...it also has some remarkable successes in it. I think, considering the way it all happened, we came out with a remarkably good film and I'm very pleased to have been a part of it. It could have been better — yes! I don't ever expect to make a film

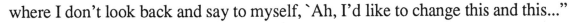

where I don't look back and say to myself, `Ah, I'd like to change this and this..."

After Roddenberry was moved off the Paramount lot, it was 1981 before the decision was made to make a *Star Trek* sequel, but a different producer, Harve Bennett, was brought in. Roddenberry was reduced to being a consultant on the films. Basically he had no creative control in that capacity, but he did advise on continuity and characterization. His participation seemed to be Paramount's way of keeping Roddenberry's name on the projects (and avoid rumors among those letter-writing STAR TREK fans) while keeping Roddenberry's participation at a minimal level. In an interview with Roddenberry in the Boston Herald on Nov. 28, 1986, the producer looked back on the experience of making *Star Trek : The Motion Picture* and compared it to his consultant position on the subsequent pictures.

"I discovered on the first movie that the director is everything. The writer-producer type, really, no one listens to him. It's just the way movies have always been made. It just about killed me on the first movie when the studio and the director made all the decisions. So I invented the term 'executive story consultant' and set the rules that they have to show me everything they do, from the first lines (through) all the rewrites and dailies." Still, it amounted to being demoted. This was underscored by the fact that Majel Barrett Roddenberry didn't play Chapel again until *Star Trek IV*, and then she saw most of her scenes wind up on the cutting room floor. When William Shatner came up with the story for *Star Trek V*, it had been approved by the studio, reworked by Shatner and Bennett and in the process of being turned into a screenplay before Roddenberry even found out about it. He raised hell and work on the script stopped until they received his input, and they did take his comments to heart and give them serious consideration as the screenplay took shape. They hadn't consulted him earlier because they'd just forgotten to.

It would be five years before Paramount saw fit to warm up to Roddenberry again, and that was when they needed him to create a new *Star Trek* television series for the studio in order to further exploit the lucrative marketability of the franchise. To show how much things could change once more, four months before Roddenberry's death in 1991, Paramount dedicated a new building on the studio lot in Roddenberry's name. If Universal Studios could have the Steven Spielberg building, then Paramount Studios could have the Gene Roddenberry Building. The winds of change blow swift and sharp, particularly in Hollywood.

Even though the first Star Trek movie returned revenues to Paramount in the neighborhood of $178 million, the $45 million cost up front still stuck in their throat. The studio began to explore less expensive avenues all of which excluded Gene Roddenberry's participation.

TWO: THE WRATH OF KHAN

In 1982, the second *Star Trek* feature, *Star Trek II: The Wrath of Khan* redressed the failing of its predecessor. Unlike STAR TREK—THE MOTION PICTURE, it contained a strong, engaging plot, plenty of action, a powerful nemesis, dramatic relationships, a famous controversy— and a notorious continuity glitch.

Although Gene Roddenberry had remained in his office on the Paramount lot writing a sequel to *Star Trek: The Motion Picture* until July of 1980, Paramount rejected his script and closed his office Not only was Roddenberry off the Paramount payroll, but the studio shelved plans for a sequel, and didn't revive them until 1981

Hoping to avoid a repeat of the huge cost over-runs and the critical failure of *Star Trek: The Motion Picture*, Paramount called in television producer Harve Bennett. He had produced *The Mod Squad, The Six Million Dollar Man* and *The Bionic Woman.*`1 Z Ç\? As a child, Bennett had even achieved some acclaim as one of the "Quiz Kids" on that early game show.

When Barry Diller, and Gulf & Western chief Charles Bludhorn, asked Bennett what he thought of the first *Star Trek* feature, Bennett admitted that he thought it was terribly boring. Bludhorn asked if Bennett could make a better movie; Bennett said yes. Bludhorn asked: "For less than forty-five f****** million dollars?"

"Where I come from," replied Bennett, "I can make four movies for that." And, in fact, Harve Bennett would wind up making *Star Treks II, III* and *IV* for roughly the same amount of money it took to produce the first feature alone. Clearly, he was the right man for the job.

Even so, Bennett had some misgivings at first, claiming, in the official *Star Trek II* book, that, "My first gut reaction was negative because I didn't want to do somebody else's legend. I had just come to Paramount. I had a track record of some size, and what appealed to me was its potential as my first feature picture. For some reason or another, I had never done a feature picture.

"I really went right past the fact that I would have to do an enormous amount of homework, from my own standards, not for anybody else's, in order to truly digest and be respectful to the material. This is a compulsion that's mine. A lot of people could come in and do a tap dance. One of my great strengths, and I suppose weaknesses, is that I don't like to do lip service to something that has worth. *Star Trek* is a phenomenon, is a project. . . and if nothing else, is an avenue of expression in a medium that was getting dryer and dryer and dryer. . . I think it is not illogical that *Star Trek* reruns, during the 1970s, fulfilled a need that network television was not fulfilling. My own network television days during that time were successful enough, but I can't tell you that *The Six Million Dollar Man* fulfilled a deep, philosophical satisfaction for me. It was a job well done, it was a yarn well told; I would never think of doing a feature picture about *The Six Million Dollar Man*. That I would turn down." Fortunately, Harve Bennett did not turn down the challenge of producing *Star Trek II*.

Comments on this project were heard early in 1980, when Leonard Nimoy, promoting his then-current television movie *Seizure: The Kathy Morris Story* (in which he played a neurosurgeon involved in a serious brain surgery case) expressed a few off-the-cuff thoughts on *Star Trek* and its future, from an Associated Press wire service report dated January 1, 1980:

"There is nothing definite yet, but I gather there's a lot of conversation at Paramount about what to do with *Star Trek* next." As for his legendary reticence to play Spock, Nimoy commented, "Some people have a conception that I have trouble playing other characters, that I'm too identified with Spock. It's no problem. It would probably be more dramatic to say it is.

"When I work in the theatre, I can feel it in the first few minutes on stage. Particularly from people who have seen me in *Star Trek*. They're trying to focus on Spock and what I'm going to be doing.

"When I played Sherlock Holmes, he was a character very close to Spock because of his logical deductions. But there was no problem."

Despite these protestations, Nimoy was not too keen on reprising the role of Spock. A great deal of his reasons were derived from the fact that the shooting of *Star Trek: The Motion Picture* was a harried and unpleasant experience. The producers, he felt, had not used the characters or concepts well, and it was only with extreme reluctance that he approached a second *Star Trek* movie. Although he will not admit it today, Nimoy was the originator of the idea to kill off Spock in the second feature. This was confirmed by Gene Roddenberry in the public talk he gave on March 30, 1988 at the Museum of Broadcasting in Los Angeles. (On the other hand, screenwriter Jack B. Sowards claimed to have pitched the idea himself, and in yet another interview, Harve Bennett has claimed credit for the idea.) At any rate, the idea did not give Nimoy much pause at all. Perhaps in shedding Spock for good, he might be able to pursue other career goals.

News of this leaked out early and caused great consternation among diehard *Star Trek* fans. Gene Roddenberry was actually instrumental in seeing that news of this got out. At a convention in 1981, Roddenberry's personal assistant, Susan Sackett stated that Harve Bennett had told her that Spock would be killed off and that it was supposed to be a secret. Sackett stated publicly, "Gene hates the idea because what happens if you want to use the character again later? You know, you're going to have to resurrect him. He's supposed to be dead. Gene is against it. It just doesn't make any sense; there's no need for it, really." She pointed out that Roddenberry had been asked about the rumor at a convention in Chicago, so the secret was out. Sackett promised that Roddenberry would fight to have that taken out of the script. "So if you don't care for that idea," Sackett added, "it's up to you to try to convince them." And try the fans did.

Some of them took out an ad in a major Hollywood trade paper predicting that Paramount would lose a considerable fortune, largely from a fan boycott, if they went through with what they considered murder. (Of a fictional character. . ?)

Leonard Nimoy heard of this while filming the mini-series *Marco Polo* in China, and later recalled his reaction with some bemusement:

"They took it upon themselves to do some 'arithmetic' and placed an ad in the trade papers saying, 'Why does Paramount want to lose eighteen million dollars?' I found that 'information' on the front page of an Asian edition of *The Wall Street Journal*, while I was in Beijing, China, shooting *Marco Polo*. It was very flattering to read about myself in China. But I also realized that a self-appointed crusade group was, in effect, trying to dictate what should happen dramatically in a given artistic demeanor.

"When those same people finally saw the movie, they were very moved and touched by it. They came away deeply satisfied, having had a terrific experience. They told us, 'Gee, we didn't realize it would be done that way.' They could have saved themselves and us a great deal of aggravation if they had only been patient." [*Starlog*, July 1984]

Indeed, these fan forebodings of doom for the *Star Trek* film series proved to be light-years off the mark.

For one thing, Paramount kept tight reigns on *Star Trek II*'s budget; it only cost thirteen million to make, less than a third of the maximum estimates of the first film's cost; on the other hand, it grossed eighty million dollars in its initial domestic release alone. Paramount definitely made a big time profit on *Star Trek II: The Wrath of Khan*.

A great deal of this was a result of the guiding hand of producer Harve Bennett. "It was fate that led me to this film," mused Bennett in a 1982 interview. It was largely the result of his long-time relationship with a woman who was a *Star Trek* aficionado. "During our long time together," the producer/writer recalled, "I've been force-fed *Star Trek* re-runs. Literally. She'd be sitting there in front of her TV set and I'd be moaning, 'How many times do we have to see these things?'

"Since I always was being told to shut up during the seventeenth showing of 'The Tholian Web,' I finally gave in and started watching. I became hooked. I became fascinated by the show!

"You see, although I'd never watched it before, I've always had sort of a peripheral involvement with it. My first successful show was *The Mod Squad*. It competed with Trek one season. We even filmed on the same lot. I used to see Leonard [Nimoy] walking by with his ears on but I never actually saw his work.

"I knew Roddenberry but had never worked with him. The times we met I liked him a lot. For some odd reason, I've always been drawn to paramilitary types. I'm a pilot. Gene was a pilot. One thing I've always perceived in *Star Trek* was the fine hand of the odd paramilitary mind that was trying to preach peace. That's a very interesting effect, rivalled in intensity only by the feelings of, let's say, a reformed drunk. You've seen the horror. Now, you want to save others from it."

Bennett also had a very close relationship with the late Gene Coon as well. Coon had been the line producer for the original STAR TREK television series. Gene Coon was an ex-Marine who believed in preaching the horrors of war from the point of view of someone who had been there.

Bennett thought the first movie was boring and believed that at the very least, he could make a film which wouldn't be dull. He began watching *Star Trek* from a scholastic point of view, taking several episodes into a projection room and screening them to develop a feel for the material. It was out of those viewings that the film was born. Bennett was particularly drawn to the episode "Space Seed," about a genetic superman named Khan who attempts to take over the Enterprise. He felt that there was magic to that confrontation between Kirk and the man from the 20th century.

Bennett found it was an uphill battle to shape a sequel of a motion picture which had met with mixed reviews from fans and critics alike. The first obstacle was that *Star Trek: The Motion Picture* had left *Star Trek* behind. He believed that by being more faithful to the type of STAR TREK that Roddenberry had done in the sixties would win back the favor of the fans.

Bennett also told *Cinefantastique* in 1991 about a key decision on his part to revitalize the Trek movies: don't hide the fact that the actors are getting older. "I am the same age as Shatner, and was going through my own time of change. I wouldn't have dared trying to look like I was twenty-five, and I was aware of how silly Bill [Shatner] looked radiating this gauzy look [in the flatteringly-shot first *Trek* picture]. Even Leonard had too much makeup— he had Lillian Gish lips. I decided *Star Trek II* was going to be gritty, about people aging."

The film also introduced a new character, the half-Romulan, half-Vulcan Saavik, played by newcomer Kirstie Alley. In Hollywood just over a year at the time, she had been a *Star Trek* fan as a child and used to imitate Spock. She did all her old Spock routines when auditioning for the part. Nicholas Meyer observed that she moved exactly like Nimoy and gave her the role.

Although all reference to Saavik being half-Romulan was cut from the film in final editing, Alley was very conscious of this aspect of the character. "We really had to work on it so that I could be sensitive and let the Romulan part of her come out a little bit. That's why the tears near the end. I was very sad. I would have cried standing at the end of that, even if I wasn't supposed to. It was very touching." An early trailer for *Star Trek II* included a conversation in which Spock was talking to Kirk about Saavik being half-Romulan, so such footage had indeed been filmed. Vonda McIntyre developed the background of Saavik in some detail for the novelization of *The Wrath of Khan*.

Gene Roddenberry, the creator of *Star Trek*, was somewhat out of the picture at this point, serving only as a "consultant" to the film. "Since [Gene] wasn't producing this film, there were some strained feelings at first. Later, he really got into it. I think we now have a very healthy respect for each other. He gave a lovely speech in the projection room one day about how proud he was to be associated with this film," Bennett stated in 1982.

Using Harve Bennett's ideas as his springboard, writer Jack B. Sowards worked out the final screenplay. Sowards recalled that he landed the writing gig for *Star Trek II* when Harve Bennett asked him if he knew much about *Star Trek*. Recalled Sowards in a 1983 Starlog interview: "I lied and said 'Everything!' "

Sowards also takes credit for being the first to suggest the death of a major character.

"I went in for the first story conference on December 4, 1980 with Harve Bennett. He said, 'Everyone's back except Leonard.' I said, 'Call him and ask how he'd like to play his death scene.' Harve did [and] Leonard said, 'I'd love to.' " Interestingly, back when Roddenberry was negotiating with Paramount to make the first *Star Trek* motion picture, the studio wanted to kill off all the main characters and replace them with new, younger stars, a position that *Star Trek's* creator adamantly opposed.

Sowards was determined, like everyone else involved in this project, to avoid the pitfalls of the previous film. "We watched *Star Trek* again and again and again. I think they got carried away with the special effects, and I don't think they had a good people story. It was a magnificent attempt, but it was wrong, that's all. It was like a family reunion: nobody did anything but stand and pose for the camera."

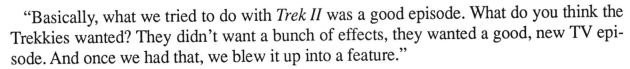

"Basically, what we tried to do with *Trek II* was a good episode. What do you think the Trekkies wanted? They didn't want a bunch of effects, they wanted a good, new TV episode. And once we had that, we blew it up into a feature."

All Sowards had to build this "good episode" out of was a handful of ideas handed him by Harve Bennett.

"Basically, he had Khan's return, the relationship between David and his mother, and a 'problem' somewhere in the universe involving Kirk that Khan would also become involved with."

Soward's script would greatly resemble the completed film as it is known today, but it had some elements— most notably psychic powers for Khan— which did not survive the final cut. Sowards did try to keep in line with Gene Roddenberry's original *Star Trek* concept, and constantly communicated with Roddenberry throughout the writing of the screenplay. "You can't do *Star Trek* without Gene. We sent most of the stuff we developed on paper to him and he sent us his notes about it. Let's face it, Gene Roddenberry is the daddy of the whole thing!"

In explaining one aspect of the script Soward's agreed to fix, the writer stated, "Apparently, we violated some Law of the Universe, the Primary Rule. I don't remember what it was, but we corrected it." Sowards was obviously speaking of the Prime Directive, something that Kirk violated frequently in the original television series.

With the first draft script ready to go, it was time to get the cast together once more. The process of rounding up all the original crew certainly posed some difficulties because the script didn't please everybody. George Takei expressed reluctance about signing because he didn't want to just be a bus driver in space again. Finally a scene was found for him which satisfied George enough to sign on, so the entire cast was reunited once again.

Walter Koenig, who had a very good scene with Ricardo Montalban in the film, neglected to mention that this big scene with Khan was in a sense impossible. Khan recognizes Chekov— who was not a character on *Star Trek* at the time of the first season's "Space Seed" episode, the forerunner of *The Wrath of Khan*. In script consultations, Gene Roddenberry actually pointed this out to Harve Bennett and director Nicholas Meyer, but was told that it was a minor point that no one would notice. Roddenberry felt vindicated when Paramount received hundreds of letters from fans pointing out this continuity glitch.

Ricardo Montalban was crucial to the success of this feature. After all, he played Khan Noonian Singh the first time around. Fortunately, Montalban had fond memories of his guest appearance on the original *Star Trek* television series. Also, when he learned that Nicholas Meyer would be the director, any remaining qualms about repeating the role were removed, as he recalled in a September 1982 interview with *Starlog* magazine: "It was a very happy company and everybody was very cordial, very nice. All the regulars were wonderful to me, most helpful, and I loved it."

"I thought the character of Khan was wonderful. I thought it was well-written, it had an interesting concept, and I was delighted it was offered to me. I still get fan mail from it. . . people remembered this Khan character whenever I talk about having done a *Star Trek*."

Then, after having agreed to play Khan again, Ricardo Montalban set about examining what his approach to the character had been, fifteen years earlier:

"He was an overly ambitious man that had dimension. Sometimes when you read a villain, he's a villain through and through. But this man had facets. He was genetically engineered with mental and physical superiority, and he uses that superiority to conquer. On the other hand, he falls in love. He takes his girl as his wife when he goes into exile. It was a love that was very real; it humanized the character for me. The dialogue was written interestingly. It fit the character.

"I asked Harve Bennett to send me a tape of the original episode and I ran it one Saturday morning. I ran it all morning, probably four times. I tried to recapture what highly delineated the character then. What did I bring to that character back then? What were the thoughts? What were the shadings, the colorations I gave the man? I tried to draw a portrait of what I had done, inwardly. Little by little, I did recall my thought process. Having that thought pattern working for me, and having seen the script years later, all I had to add were the years of frustration from exile and the age and so forth— it all started to fall into place. Because of all the circumstances and what happened, pain can change a man. Therefore, his wrath is right and when you have wrath there is a certain amount of irrationality. But I didn't intend on making him insane. He's guided by this incredible vengeance, this sense of injustice he feels has been done to him."

Ricardo Montalban breathed new life into Khan, making him the most memorable of the *Star Trek* movie villains, even after six films have joined the pantheon.

Hedging their bets over the Spock issue, the studio introduced a new (backup?) Vulcan character, Lieutenant Saavik, portrayed by Kirstie Alley. As director, they had hired Nicholas Meyer, a successful novelist (*The Seven Per Cent Solution*) turned movie director (*Time After Time* and the TV-movie *The Day After*), who brought a deft directorial hand and a humanizing touch to the proceedings. Meyer entered the world of film by way of Paramount Pictures' publicity department. He worked as the unit publicist for *Love Story* which led to a deal writing the book about the making of that film; Meyer took the proceeds and made his way to Hollywood, where he started work in the story department at Warner Brothers.

"In college," Meyer recalled in an interview in ENTERPRISE INCIDENTS, "I learned that I wasn't a very good actor. I then shifted my goal because in the process of learning that I wasn't a good actor, I learned what interested me more was what the director did. I then said, 'Yes, this is what I really wish to be.' So I shifted my goal to directing when I was about eighteen years old. However, I think my unconscious goal. . . was to be a writer, or more generically, a storyteller— a teller of tales— a very old profession— possibly the second oldest. Ever since I was five years old, I had been scribbling down stories. It never occurred to me to formulate this into a coherent expression of goals: 'I want to be a writer.' The cache of being a writer never occurred to me. But a writer, good, bad or indifferent, is what I am. And that's what I am first.

"Directing is a group, a societal, collaborative, familial exercise over which your control is comparatively limited by your abilities but also by your budget, the nature of the collaboration, the amount of time you have, etcetera."

Altering the color scheme of the Enterprise sets and adding such sensible, human details as "no smoking" signs and fire extinguishers as well, Meyer was determined not to repeat the mistakes of the first movie. Still, he was a bit surprise to be involved at all.

In an interview in *Enterprise* #10 (April 1985), Meyer explained how he became attached to *Star Trek II.*

"A friend of mine, named Karen Moore, who at the time was working for Paramount, was visiting me one night. I had done nothing since *Time After Time.* I had turned down a lot of stuff, trying to get my own script for a movie called *Conjuring* made. So I wrote the book *Confessions Of A Homing Pigeon,* which came out in October '81. This was just before that. . .

"Karen said to me, 'You know, if you want to learn how to direct movies, you should direct.' She suggested the *Star Trek* 2 movie and said that the two guys producing it were very nice. They sent me the script, which I loved. I met Harve [Bennett] and Bob [Sallin] and I thought they were wonderful. I haven't changed my views since! As far as making the film was concerned, I could not have been better partnered to not look like a fool because of the expertise and support I was given."

In another interview, in the February 1984 issue of *Enterprise Incidents,* Meyer went on to say, "Well, I never was anybody's first choice. I don't know how far down the line I was. I accepted it because I wanted to make *Conjuring* and they said, 'Make a big hit movie and you can do what you want. ' Then I saw the first *Star Trek* film and I thought [that] I could make a better movie than this. That was good reason to do the sequel in that the first one had not fulfilled its promise. It had not been what it ought to be or what it could have been."

The thing that he liked about the TV series, and what he thought made it special, was the people. He wanted to take them seriously in his film, or at least more seriously than they'd ever been taken before. Thus the main subtext of the film would be aging and death.

"There was a lot of pressure to back off [from the downbeat ending]. They always [go] for the jugular when they want you to change things. They go for the one thing that makes it distinguished or distinctive. I said, let's be real, and everybody said, oh yes, let's be real. Then we got into how real real is. Then there was a flurry of back-pedaling about this and that, and you're going to kill the series. My interest was not in the series. My interest was in this movie, to make it the best because it has my name on it, and for me there was the task of making the people real."

Meyer felt that the actors had played these parts too much and had, in a sense, got a lock on them which was fixed into a television sensibility in which everything always ends up at the end of the hour back where it was at the beginning of the hour. Aging and death, Kirk wearing glasses, was a bit of a shock to them at the beginning, but when they got to know the director and trust him, it became an enjoyable challenge. Meyer ultimately felt that the actors breathed new life into those roles, and he truly came to love them and enjoy working with them.

"One of the reasons I did this picture was to make the people real. That's all that interests me," Meyer stated. "Why can't Captain Kirk read a book? Why can't he do anything that we do? One of the things I had to back off on was having him smoke. There's a sign in the simulator saying 'No Smoking On The Bridge.' Somebody said they're not going to smoke in the 23rd Century. I said, 'Why not?' They've been smoking for four hundred years. No one has given it up despite the Surgeon General's warning. Why can't they drink a cup of coffee? I keep thinking that the bridge was like the bridge of a destroyer with fog around and guys in pea jackets coming up with coffee. We decided they probably snorted Brim. But why can't Kirk read a book? And then the book I chose for him to read became loaded with significance."

Meyer was also intrigued to learn that the character of James T. Kirk had been based on that of Captain Horatio Hornblower. Shatner told him this and both the actor and Meyer were excited by this as each had independently viewed the character in exactly the same way. Meyer even made everyone watch the old Captain Hornlower movie directed by Raoul Walsh. He admitted that the midshipman who became Scotty's nephew in The Wrath of Khan was stolen out of the Hornblower film.

Such off-the-cuff improvements met with the approval of screenwriter Jack B. Sowards, who felt that spontaneous changes on the set make the show breathe, and give it life rather than freezing it in ice.

Special effects this time around were provided by Industrial Light and Magic, the effects company that grew out of George Lucas' *Star Wars* projects.

Art director Mike Minor approached the new film by striving to address the failings of *Star Trek: The Motion Picture.*

"I thought the first movie was pretty washed out, visually," he stated in a 1982 *Starlog* interview. "It had no heart. Part of that can be traced back to the design element. During the first picture, all the sets were buttoned up. In other words, the bridge was built as one, solid structure. It could never be opened up to get a camera into it for a better angle. That camera was going to be inside a real ship and we were going to wander around the vessel with it in a very slow, stately manner. That situation forced the filmmakers into a corner. They had to use very dim lighting on the sets. They couldn't let the proper amount of lights onto them because everything was so cramped."

Plus, they had to dim the lighting even further in order to record all the console screen designs. In the first movie, the screens were eight millimeter and sixteen millimeter film loops being projected onto monitors. The dull lighting gave the whole ship a rather gloomy, dull atmosphere.

Like many people involved in special effects, Minor had a long-standing soft spot in his heart for *Star Trek*, and in fact had worked on the old TV series during its third season. "Our technical consultant, Dr. Richard Green, is also a real fan. So is Gayne Rescher, the director of photography. He really committed himself to the picture, and even came in two weeks early to work with Nick Meyer, figuring out how to shoot the bridge. People are going to notice how much more interesting the photography is in this picture because the camera is always in motion."

For *Star Trek II*, things were restored to their former nature, as Minor explained. "They made the bridge set totally wild. All eleven sections of the bridge, as originally designed by Joe Jennings back in 1977, were unbuttoned, disconnected. We could pull sections out like you pull out slices of pie and get that camera in there on a twelve-foot crane. We could get that camera to swoop and dive and dolly and truck. There's a lot more action aboard the ship this time out. You race down the corridors. You have the image of the *Enterprise* whizzing right past you.

"[The] *Enterprise* can really be difficult to deal with in space. It's a sculpture, really. It's not a junk ship. The Lucas ships in *Star Wars* all have layer upon layer of stuff glued on top of them. It may be visually thrilling, but it's not particularly accurate. The *Enterprise* is an aerodynamic shape. If you film it wrong, it can look silly."

Because of time and budgetary considerations, they were forced to make quite a lot of cuts. Their original design budget came in for less than a million dollars, but Paramount told them to shave that by a third. They were all so into the *Star Trek* idea that they found ways to work around any and all difficulties.

Lee Cole, the graphics expert who worked with Mike Minor on the film, agreed. "Because of the budget, we recycled every fragment of the old sets for this movie. That was quite a challenge. In this movie, the *Enterprise* has a different look.

"We cut the Klingon set from the first film in half. Part of it is now the torpedo room aboard the *Enterprise*. Part of it became the transporter room of the space station. I very carefully had to cut out all the Klingon writing."

For all the budgetary restrictions on this particular film project, Cole pointed out that Paramount probably got more for their money than on the previous *Star Trek* feature. "You see more of the ship in this film. You see the torpedo room. You see the inner workings of sick bay. You see the living quarters. We also improved the bridge quite a bit. We added a lot of detailing. Nick Meyer loved little flashing lights and do-dads."

They also altered the video screens on the bridge to remove all the rear-projection film set-ups that the first movie had put there. In their place they installed real video units. That was tough because they had to custom build a video system.

They redesigned the *Enterprise* for the *Reliant.* by essentially giving the *Enterprise* a roll bar. The *Reliant* is designed to look like an earlier model starship because the *Enterprise* is supposed to be the state of the art in terms of starship technology.

Effects supervisor Ken Ralston was less than sanguine about the hardware used in the film. "I hate the Enterprise model," he swore. "I think it's made out of lead. It took eight guys to mount it for a shot and a forklift to move it around.

"The ship won't look any different on the screen," Ralston continued, referring to the extra detailing and rougher texture he added to the leftover (and weighty) model. "The iridescence effect still works, but having a little relief on the surface made things easier on us. We didn't have to horse around with the lighting to get rid of gloss."

Ralston admitted that he never really cared for the original design of the Enterprise because it was a shape that does not lend itself easily to looking good in the frame. On the other hand Ralston felt that the Reliant is a nice, squat contraption that looked a lot more believable. He felt that the Reliant takes the best of the Enterprise, rearranges it, and adds a few good things of its own.

Actually, it was Mike Minor who came up with a key element of *Star Trek II's* plot, although he did not receive any writing credit. "Harve wanted something uplifting," Minor told *Cinefantastique* magazine in the July-August 1982 issue, "something that would be as fundamental in the Twenty-third century as the discovery of recombinant DNA is in our time. Then something just came to me, and I said, 'Terraforming.' Harve asked, 'What's that?' and I told him it was the altering of existing planets to conditions which are compatible to human life. I suggested a plot, just making it up in my head while talking on the phone. . . the Federation had developed a way of engineering the planetary evolution of a body in space on such a rapid scale that instead of eons you have events taking place in months or years. You pick a dead world or an inhospitable gas planet, and you change its genetic matrix or code, thereby speeding up time. This, of course, is a terrible weapon; suppose you trained it on a planet filled with people and speeded up its evolution. You could destroy the planet and every life form on it. The Federation is involved with playing God, but at the same time, trying to take barren dead worlds and convert them into lovely worlds. Harve liked the idea. At the story conference the next day, he came over, hugged me, and said, 'You saved *Star Trek!*' "

Production began on November 9, 1981 and wrapped on January 2, 1982; after post production work was completed, the film was released on June 4, 1982. Meyer encountered some interesting problems during this period. There were the technical demands of working on the set, which is a difficult set to shoot. Most of the action takes place on the bridge, which is a three-hundred-and-sixty degree set. Plus, the bridge set was hard to light. "Making the film was very, very hard," Meyer told ENTERPRISE INCIDENTS in the February 1984 issues. "One of the hardest things I ever did. I think one of the things that made it so much harder than it needed to be was that before we rolled the camera, Paramount had booked this movie into umpteen hundred theaters on June 4 [1982], which I didn't know. That didn't give much post-production time, the time used to complete the film. I can only contrast it wit*Time After Time*. We finished shooting that movie Thanksgiving 1978 and the movie was released in October 1979, so I had, in effect, a year to finish the film. Five months to edit it. Editing is where films really get made. Dailies are like sentences in a book which hasn't been written yet. Editing is that process of trial and error, and also of contemplation. A five-month editing period is very useful for a movie. You can try things and change things and experiment and play around. I had a year to do it."

They finished shooting *The Wrath of Khan* February first, 1982. Then the special effects had to be shot during the day and edited at night. Normally Industrial Light & Magic would take a year to do something as demanding as this motion picture was, but they only had a month, and that left Meyer only two and a half weeks to edit the movie in time for the summer release date. In order to give himself a few more weeks to work with, when he was shooting the principal photography with the actors, Meyer shot during the day and edited at night and on weekends. That meant that for more than six weeks, the director pretty much never saw the light of day.

"I would go to work at about five-thirty or six o'clock, before the sun had come up. I would eat lunch in a dark theatre looking at my dailies, so I'd never see the sunshine then. At night we would come out of the soundstages and I would go off to the editing room, by which time it was dark. On weekends I would also get up before sunrise and go down to the editing room. I wondered whether I would physically be able to stand it because I was putting in eighteen-hour days, seven days a week. That part of it was not fun. The shooting of it continued to be fun, but that was played against exhaustion."

Meyer vowed that he will never again make a movie in which he doesn't know beforehand that he has enough time to finish it. "We were such a photo-finish that we started printing the film— to make sixteen hundred prints takes three weeks in itself so count backwards from June fourth to May tenth or something like that— and then there were special effects coming in. ILM would send us down pieces of film with a label on it, shot

36A, and we would have to match that angle with shooting it. My cut of the movie when it was first put together was a fifty-percent 'scene missing' or 'insert missing.' Kirk would say 'Fire,' and then 'scene missing.' It made it very hard to tell about the movie.

"Basically, changing the film is no big deal," Meyer continued. "Theoretically, you could keep changing right up until you print. But you will affect the sound. Sound effects are made up of many tracks. So if a reel of film is a thousand feet long and somewhere four hundred and thirty-odd feet in, somebody knocks on the door, there's a separate reel of film that is black for four hundred and thirty-seven feet, there's a knock, and black for the rest of the reel. That is completely separate. Ray guns or whatever we're talking about are all on separate tracks. So you have as many as fifty or more separate sound-tracks for the same reel of film. So what sound people keep hounding you for are what are called 'locked reels,' finished reels. My problem was that I was deprived of that period called contemplation, when you play with the film. If you suddenly have an Epiphany, 'Gee, I know now I can make it ten times better. Just remove thirteen frames from Spock opening his eyes so he opens them a little faster,' or something at the beginning of the movie— that's hell to do that, and it costs a fortune.

"The whole history is that this movie started out as nothing. This movie was to be made by the television department for a song and a prayer. They felt as though you've got these sets, they're all standing. . . they didn't realize that the sets had been completely vandalized; they had been completely ripped off. There was nothing. . . You've got all these sets, so let's get the actors and run them out in front and let *Star Trek* money-making machine do its thing. They didn't really care about the movie, and that was reflected in the budget. They felt we could score it with a synthesizer, that would be all right. I said, why not a kazoo?"

Meyer found that the process of making this film was that of turning the studio around and convincing them that Meyer and his people were going to do a class act and an event. Slowly, inch-by-inch, piccolo by violin, cello by trumpet, they retreated and gave ground. They said, 'Why can't we do tracking?' Tracking is taking existing music from their library and laying it in some place else.

"Now, I'm not a person who thinks you have to spend a lot of money necessarily to make something good," Meyer continued, "but you have to be able to afford what you are convinced you need. I was convinced that we needed a large orchestra for this. On the other hand, I was not convinced that we needed to spend forty thousand for a composer, so we listened to a cassette. I met with James Horner and I really liked him a lot. He was real keen to do it. We were not real *Star Trek* fans when we started, but we became con-verted as time went on.

Originally, Spock's death occurred midway through the movie, a placement altered by director Meyer:

"I said he has to die at the end because there is no way you're going to top it. the movie is going to be anticlimactic if he dies in the middle, so I said he should die at the end." Walter Koenig has stated that he suggested that Spock should die at the end, as early drafts of the script had Spock dying in the middle of the story.

Once the film was completed, Meyer found himself dealing with an unasked-for controversy regarding the subtitle of *Star Trek II*. Originally the film had been called *Star Trek II: The Undiscovered Country*. The "undiscovered country" in the title referred to death, whereas in *Star Trek VI* it means the future. But Paramount decided to change it to *The Vengeance of Khan*. Meyer was annoyed by this decision because the title had been changed by an executive in New York who hadn't even seen the picture yet. The executive in question defended his decision by saying that it made for a more exciting title. Meyer was quick to point out a bit of a problem. George Lucas was making a film with the announced title of Revenge of the Jedi and he didn't think that the producer would care to hear of a similarly titled film being released first. So at the last minute they changed the title to *The Wrath of Khan*, which Meyer though was even worse. Meyer says he can still remember Barry Diller, then head of Paramount, a week before the movie opened, fuming, saying, 'We never should have called this picture *The Wrath of Khan*. Whose idea was it? People don't even know what that word means!'

Of course, Chekov was not yet assigned to Terrell's command when the events of the first season *Star Trek* episode "Space Seed" occurred; although he would probably be aware of those events, this does not explain how the suddenly returning Khan Noonian Singh (Ricardo Montalban) recognizes Chekov as a former *Enterprise* officer. This is an unfortunate continuity glitch, but one which, if corrected, would have cost Chekov his big scene. While Walter Koenig realized this, he wasn't about to make an observation which would possibly cause the script to be altered so that a different character would have these scenes. The supporting cast in the *Star Trek* films were given little enough to do as it was.

Jack B. Sowards' original version of the story takes a slightly different tack. Sowards' approach to the confrontation between Khan and Kirk was a bit more intimate than the way it wound up on screen. "One of the things I had with the mystic approach— which I liked better than the way it was done in the film— was that Khan actually met Kirk face-to-face in the Genesis cave. I like that better than the two always being off in space together making phone calls."

The mystic approach refers to Sowards' concept that Khan would have developed psychic powers of a sort during his lengthy

exile. In the earlier screenplay version, Khan beams down to face Kirk in the Genesis cave. Sowards had given Khan certain powers, such as creating hallucinations. When Khan arrives, he gestures at David, who rolls up into a ball of pain. Kirk tells David, 'It's all in your mind, David. None of this is really happening. Fight it.' Suddenly, Kirk and Khan appear on a beach, armed with these scorpion-tipped Romulan whips. They fight with those to the point where Kirk is almost beaten. Then, Khan beats up Kirk once again, inflicting terrible punishment, while Kirk is saying the whole time, 'This isn't really happening.' Khan is cutting him up and asking, 'How are you feeling Kirk?' When Khan can't win through force of will he returns to his ship.

As the film was shot, however, Khan does not beam down; it seems that he and Kirk are destined to fight it out by telephone. Jack B. Sowards, upon seeing how the death of Spock was shot, remembered that he had written it somewhat differently. "Someone jazzed it up," he commented. "I sent Spock into the room, which was bathed in a deep blue, cobalt light. In the movie, you see things spurting out at him and all that. The way I had it, he walks into the room just as he would walk onto the bridge, knowing from the moment he steps inside that he's dying. It was just the fact that you knew he was dying. While he was in there, adjusting knobs and pressing buttons as if he was cooking his breakfast. . . I didn't have all that stuff spurting out." [*Starlog*, February 1983]

Leonard Nimoy, on the other hand, was quite pleased with the final result. He found himself being moved by the scene early, at about the point where Kirk says to Scott that you have to get us out of here in three minutes or we're all dead. You see Spock hear that and react, and Nimoy was already feeling emotional about what's coming. Nimoy actually came within a hair's breadth of walking off the lot rather than playing the scene. The day he shot the scene he was very edgy about it and scared of playing it—almost looking for an excuse not to. It was a very tense time and he still feels that way upon seeing it now.

A full funeral is given, and Spock's body is launched in a photon torpedo casing heading for the newly born Genesis planet below. It comes to rest in the lush jungle foliage of the newborn world. Originally this script called for a prayer to be said—a Christian prayer at a Vulcan funeral. Roddenberry strongly objected to this notion and it was finally dropped from the script. Gene Roddenberry had long maintained that the Enterprise would be a ship of many cultures and faiths, and certainly a Vulcan funeral wouldn't have a Christian prayer, in spite of Spock's half-human heritage.

The screenwriter, Jack Sowards, didn't like Saavik crying at the funeral, though, and neither did Roddenberry, even if Saavik was supposed to be half-Romulan. They thought that someone must have told her to do it. But Alley said that it was her own idea to bring her Romulan side to the surface in the face of Spock's death.

But Sowards' reaction to the funeral scene was mild compared to that of composer James Horner, who didn't feel that a certain piece of music was appropriate for the funeral scene. Why in the world, he wondered, would they play "Amazing Grace" at a Vulcan's funeral? "I never wanted to use it! I begged, begged, 'Please don't make me use

'Amazing Grace.' It was the only battle in the film I lost. They all seemed to feel that 'Amazing Grace' was the only thing to make them happy. It was fifteen seconds— I just did it. It had already been shot, and I had to match it. Then I had the additional problem: would I continue to use the bagpipe music outside the ship or would I switch to orchestral music? My feeling was to do something very ethereal.

"The bagpipes were the wrong move. They sound like bleating goats. What you heard in the film originally was just the bagpipe alone. [The studio] had a problem in the previews with people laughing at the sound. The producers wanted the bagpipe sound changed. The only thing I could do about the curse of the bagpipes was [to] put in a [musical] cue. . . I had this strange chord that hangs over the whole scene; it did quite a bit, but doesn't solve the problem completely. You still get people laughing at the bagpipes. It was, perhaps, a slight miscalculation, but it's one of those things that you're not going to know if it works until you do it with an audience."

Credit for the bagpipes goes to Harve Bennett, who said that he once went to a High Episcopal service held in St. James Cathedral for a friend in the British diplomatic corps. At the end of the service, a lone bagpiper walked down the aisle of the nave, turned, and played 'Amazing Grace' [a traditional Scottish burial march]. He decided that since Scotty was there at the funeral that he could be playing bagpipes. Unfortunately, attempts to have James Doohan finger the pipes wound up on the cutting room floor, and few viewers realize that Scotty is supposed to be playing the pipes.

Still, Horner, whose previous musical scores included such movies as *The Lady In Red*, Roger Corman's *Up From The Depths, Humanoids From The Deep, Battle Beyond the Stars*, Oliver Stone's *The Hand, Deadly Blessing* and *Wolfen*, finally compromised on this point, largely because of time restrictions. "I had four and a half weeks to do the score. [The movie] had a pushed production schedule; they had to be in the theaters by June 4th, and they started dubbing April 9th. I had to have the music available by April 15th."

Bagpipes and old hymns notwithstanding, Horner was largely pleased with this work experience, and managed to interpolate bits of a familiar musical sequence into the score for *Star Trek II*. "I didn't think there would be any place for [the *Star Trek* theme] in the film. I said I'd think about it. [But] I worked out a way to use the *Star Trek* fanfare, which I used about four or five times, and it works very well. I had always wanted to use that fanfare, actually. Unlike the first *Star Trek* film [scored by Jerry Goldsmith], I wanted right from the start to grip the audience and tell them that they were going to see *Star Trek*. And there are only two things that can do that, either the *Enterprise*, or the *Star Trek* fanfare. The fanfare draws you in immediately— you know you're going to get a good movie."

In addition to working in the old familiar fanfare, he created new themes, particularly for one key focal character. "Spock never had a theme before, and I wanted to give him a theme to tie the whole of 'Genesis' and 'Spock' by the end of the film, so that it would all mean something. The theme for Spock, incidentally, is actually heard of at the 'leaving drydock' sequence." [*Starlog,* October 1982]

Once the film was wrapped and in the theaters, to considerable public acclaim, the cast members had a variety of feelings about the finished product. On the overwhelmingly positive side was the opinion voiced by DeForest Kelley, who felt that this was really the first Star Trek movie and that Star Trek—The Motion Picture should be ignored. Kelley felt that everything about the production and the film generated a positive feeling, unlike the first picture.

Nichelle Nichols, as well, had no complaints about her involvement in *Star Trek II*. She said that it was a very pleasant experience and that everyone knew that this picture was much more *Star Trek* than the first one was, full of much more of the intense emotion and action that fans had come to expect from *Star Trek*.

William Shatner confirmed these feelings of good will. "In the last film we were wrestling with script difficulties all through the making of the movie. The smoothness of this production added an element of good feeling among the people working on the film. It was easier on the psyche coming to work knowing that you had a finished script to work from. . . and a good one, at that." [*Starlog*, August 1982]

In the November 1982 issue of *Fantastic Films*, William Shatner was already spilling the beans about whether Nimoy would ever play Spock again, and he did this by telling a behind-the-scenes story about *Star Trek II*.

"We're in the middle of filming. We're having a ball and laughing with Nicholas Meyer, our director, pulling Nick's pants down. Things got to be fun and Leonard was joking with me. He loves Harve Bennett, the producer and everybody's so happy. So one day, I'm sitting in Leonard's dressing room and I say, 'You know, Len, this is going so well. . . gosh. . . why do you want to die?'

"Leonard looked at me. 'Who said I wanted to die?'

"I said, 'You mean you'll come back?'

" 'Yeah,' he said, 'Listen, I'm having such a good time, maybe I won't die. . . forever. . .'

"So me, the snitch, ran up to Harve Bennett and exclaimed, 'Guess what I've got to tell you!'

"Harve said, 'Go back to the set. You're on now.'

"No, I told him, you're going to want to hear this. Leonard just told me he wouldn't mind playing Spock again!

"Well, Harve fell down. I picked him up and he fell down again. He was rather over-come. That was halfway through the movie, so we had to get clever and try to make it so even though he dies, we could bring him back to life. I'm not sure who, but I surmise it was Harve and Nick who decided to put Spock's coffin down into the very device that brings life to barren objects." Shatner smiled slyly, "and we all know Leonard is barren. .

"Paramount was a little apprehensive about killing a major character," Shatner ex-plained. "They wanted to have something else they could use in case the death of Spock didn't work. No other ending was contemplated, but that last shot was kind of manipulat-ed a little bit. Instead of being shot into space, which was the original concept, it was de-cided to make the sarcophagus land in the lush fields of the Genesis effect. That was the only adjustment, but it was a key adjustment."

Meyer fought against the change, and told *Cinefantastique.* "I fought very hard to make him dead, and the shots that imply a resurrection—the vision of the casket on the genesis planet—were done over my dead body, with my strenuous objection. I objected so strenuously, and went to such lengths, that a producer on the film referred to me as morally bankrupt. He said, 'You'd walk over your mother to get this the way you want-ed,' and I said, 'You know I think you're right.' "

With such an overwhelming climax, interest was immediately focused on the next pic-ture. Was Spock *really* dead— and what part, if any, would Leonard Nimoy have in the production? He was certainly approached about it by the studio, although this in-formation was kept under wraps until Paramount devised a means of linking Nimoy with *Star Trek III*— without revealing anything about the status of Spock.

Leonard Nimoy, who may have had *some* idea of what was in the offing, was, it seems in retrospect, just a bit coy in discussing the future of the series, as well as his possible participation in future installments. "There are certainly doors available to walk through. But that's not in my hands. I can't predict what Paramount will do. I suspect they'll want to do more. We're having some conversations about doing more but nothing is hard and concrete yet. Chances are they will do something. The whole *Star Trek* thing has gone through so many bizarre twists and turns they couldn't surprise me with anything they came up with. I would think they would want to do another one— which would open in, say, a year from now."

Always intrigued by fan reactions to the rumors of Spock's death, Nimoy was now faced with the behavior of fans who were obliged to deal with their hero's death as a "real" tragedy. Some, it seems, dealt with it better than others. "There's a moment," Ni-moy recalled, "a very interesting moment to me in terms of audience reaction, when you see Spock on the floor through the glass in the distance and Kirk at the glass saying 'Spock! Spock!,' and cut back to see Spock rising. And after hearing McCoy say he's already dead, now you see him rise, I'm sure you start to wonder if maybe he's going to be okay. I think there are some in the audience who think that he's getting himself together again and is going to be okay. That we'll have some strange magical kind of explanation as to how he survived this thing. And then there are others in the audience who are very moved by it because they see it as Spock kind of recovering his dignity for his last moments with his superior officer. It's a very moving kind of thing.

"The way it's perceived by an individual in the audience depends on whether or not that individual is willing to accept the fact that Spock has died. There are people who are not going to accept it. It has been denied by many. They just don't accept it.

"It's the strangest thing. I don't know what you'd have to do to make [that scene] any more thorough or honest. But I had an experience [when] I was coming back from the East coast and I went to the airline check-in at Kennedy Airport and the lady behind the counter said, 'Mister Nimoy, did you die in the movie?'

"I said, 'You're going to have to see the picture.'

"She said, 'I did.' Now there's a case of denial. It's fascinating to me, absolute denial. I mean she just does not want to come to grips with the fact that Spock is dead. Even temporarily dead. . . I mean she just doesn't, she's so uncomfortable with the idea."

Other, more positive-thinking *Star Trek* viewers might have noticed that *Star Trek II* ended with the words which usually *opened* the television show; this time around, they were not spoken by William Shatner, but by Leonard Nimoy. "A lovely touch, isn't it?" recalled Nimoy. "That was presented to me, I think, by Harve Bennett.

"[The] words, as I spoke them, for me took on a new and possibly very interesting connotation, when [Spock] said, 'To boldly go where no man has gone before.' He could be talking about some other kind of life that he finds which we may find out about in the future. Or it may simply be his way of saying goodbye to the *Enterprise* and *Star Trek* and all that's connected with it."

"I feel that the next *Star Trek* offers a great opportunity for exploration of science fiction involved with Vulcan mysticism, Vulcan metaphysics, if you will. There's a world of ideas to be opened in terms of the Vulcan beliefs about life, death, and life— Vulcan beliefs about reincarnation or transmigration of the spirit."

After all, there was a more than subtle hint planted in the final cut of *Star Trek II*. "What was it that Spock planted in McCoy's mind when he said 'Remember'? He did the mind-meld with McCoy just before going into the chamber. Remember what?" asked Nimoy, perhaps toying with the minds of his fans. "It's obvious there's some kind of ticking clock going on in there that might be explored later. We can open that up and say, 'What is McCoy carrying around in his head that he may not even know about consciously yet that may spring to life later and be a factor in the next movie?' There's a lot of juicy stuff to contend with."

And indeed, soon enough, there *would* be a juicy story in the offing, one that audiences could really sink their teeth into; it would not be very long at all before Paramount announced their plans to film *Star Trek III: The Search For Spock*, and that the movie would involve the active participation of Leonard Nimoy. . . but not in a role that anyone would have expected him to play.

*Two views of William Shatner on the bridge
of the Enterprise at Universal Stuidos Star Trek Adventure*
PHOTO © JAMES VAN HISE

Gene Roddenberry gets his star
PHOTO © JAMES VAN HISE

Flushed from the low cost and high return of Star Trek II, Paramount decided to keep the series active. They kept the same production team who had brought the second picture to the screen, but with one important difference.

THREE: THE SEARCH FOR SPOCK

"I wasn't too keen for them to resurrect Spock. But then again, Leonard Nimoy's got to keep working. Maybe I was wrong." —Nicholas Meyer

The first problem in launching *Star Trek III* was, of course, the seemingly insurmountable fact that Spock was dead. Of course, as Nimoy's comments in the previous chapter would seem to indicate, there was always some sort of option available. And in fact, it was writer/producer Harve Bennett who came up with something resembling a notion, close to the end of *Star Trek II's* shooting schedule.

"It became my task as a writer to paint myself out of the corner that I, as a producer, had painted myself into with *The Wrath of Khan*. The studio was convinced that the film was an irrevocable downer. We felt that we could be more hopeful and ambiguous by designing the [final] ending, with the capsule landing on Genesis. . . Then we did an insert, an enhancement of something in the film, a closeup of Spock doing a mind-meld with McCoy and saying 'Remember.' Leonard asked, 'Why are we doing this?' I said, 'I don't know. I only knew that a mind melded 'remember' would be a wonderful place to start writing if I was ever to write again," Bennett stated in the December 1984 issue of *Enterprise Incidents*.

During negotiations for *Star Trek III,* Leonard Nimoy rather offhandedly suggested that he thought he could direct as well as either of his predecessors, as he knew the basic material a bit more intimately than they did. After appearing in *Star Trek: The Motion Picture* and *Star Trek II: The Wrath of Khan*, Nimoy became convinced that he could direct a *Star Trek* film that would make sense. In the January 1985 issue of Enterprise Incidents he stated that when *Star Trek III* came along, he knew Paramount would probably offer him another pay or play deal, but he pointed out that the only job they had to offer, which he might like to take a crack at, was directing.

"My feeling was that Nick Meyer was still essentially an outsider who was trying to find out how to use all of these elements that have been laying there cooking for eighteen years, and I said, 'I think I can do the job. I think I can do as well if not better.' I have some inside information on the characters that neither of them [Robert Wise, Nick Meyer] had, so I went for the brass ring and finally they said, 'Okay, let's do it.'"

In the August 4, 1983 *Los Angeles Times,* Nimoy added, "It becomes terribly frustrating when you know as much as we do about a project and you're not able to have input. Now I'll finally have the chance to express the ideas I've had about Star Trek for all those years. I dream about it—I think up ideas in the shower, or driving to the studio. It has opened a tremendous fountain of energy for me, and I'm grateful for the opportunity to express it."

So a directorial career was launched, almost by accident, since he only thought about suggesting that he direct *Star Trek III* five minutes before his meeting with the Paramount brass. Actually, Nimoy had directed before. He had two *Night Gallery* episodes and a *Mission Impossible* under his belt, along with an episode of Harve Bennett's short-lived science-fiction teen series *The Powers of Matthew Star.* He also did one episode of William Shatner's *T.J. Hooker.* As Nimoy himself told *Starlog* magazine in 1984, "Directing *Star Trek* has been in my mind since 1966. Bill Shatner and I wanted to direct episodes of the television series. We asked for that opportunity during the second and third seasons, but we met with resistance."

Of course, from a marketing standpoint alone, having Nimoy direct was a brilliant move. With Spock dead, *The Search For Spock* could be advertised using Leonard Nimoy's name— while at the same time preserving the mystery of the beloved Vulcan's ultimate fate. Nimoy's return was further brightened by a new enthusiasm fo*Star Trek* brought about by a more positive experience on the previous film.

The unpleasantness of the first feature was a matter of the past. Under Nicholas Meyer's direction, the cast regained the old camaraderie that was sadly missing from the first big-screen voyage. Nimoy summed it up best, perhaps, when he said, "For me, the film really deals with the responsibilities of friendship. The crew members are confronted with a personal decision that each must make. They set out on a personal mission, because of a hope they have. There's also a sense of [Japanese director Akira Kurosawa's] *The Seven Samurai*— a gathering of the group who will try to do the honorable thing."

But William Shatner wasn't as enthusiastic about the idea of Leonard directing because on the previous films they had been equals, supporting each other. Shatner knew that on a feature, the director is the boss during shooting and he felt as though he might lose control of the position of Kirk in the *Star Trek* setting with Leonard directing. This came to a head when an early draft of the screenplay was sent to Shatner for his input. Harve Bennett recalled what happened .

"He called and said, 'I'd like to have a meeting.' So we came over on a Sunday morning to Bill's house and there was Bill's lawyer, his agent and one guy who kept his hands over his chest. I thought maybe he was from *Hooker*—the stunt guy or something. Very intimidating. And he said, 'Are you all happy with the script?' I said, Yeah, we like it a lot. Leonard said, 'Promising, very promising.' Bill said, 'Well, I just can't do that.' The complaint was that there wasn't enough of him in the material. That he was standing by, that he wasn't leading. We said, 'Let's talk about it.' There was merit in much of what he said. He said, 'Oh, good. You other guys can leave now.' And the lawyer left and the agent left and the gunsel left, and we had five hours of intense conversation.

"You have to understand that it is not quite as selfish as it seems. This is their career. It's like a quarterback saying, 'Who's going to be blocking for me?' The actor says, 'How am I going to come off? Are they going to like me? Are they going to love me so that I can make the next picture? Being a star over a long period of time is a nerve wracking affair. So that's where his thrust was, and we had neglected to protect our star," Bennett explained.

"As soon as we got past the initial question of trust, the rest was a breeze," Nimoy added. "As soon as the cast realized that I intended to collaborate with them, rather than dictate to them, we were home free. I come from an actor's roots, so I knew what the actors wanted to contribute to the film. I have a great respect for all the *Star Trek* cast and the characters they play. . . the point is that these characters have a presence. They're treated like real people, rather than just button-pushers in the background.

"I sensed happy, productive, generous actors doing what they like to do, and feeling good about doing it. And since we finished shooting, all of the actors have responded to me with gifts and notes telling me how pleased they were with the work we did. I think the audience will recognize that rapport, because it is captured on the screen." [*Starlog*, July 1984]

Production on *Star Trek III* began on August 15, 1983. The shooting schedule was a tight forty-nine days, the budget a cool sixteen million, and the set so tightly secured that it could hold water; there were to be no advance revelations regarding this *Star Trek*. Scripts were treated chemically so that any that wound up on the black market could be traced to the parties responsible.

Eventually there were leaks, the most notable one concerning the destruction of the Starship *Enterprise*, but Nimoy and his production team ignored the fan outcry that seemed to regard the vessel as a character in its own right. "Many *Star Trek* fans want to be the first on their block to know everything before they see the film," explained the security-minded Nimoy. "To an extent, I consider that a blessing, because if they weren't interested, Paramount would have no reason to keep making these movies. On the other hand, I find that most people don't want to know. They don't want to have the surprises spoiled. I think our job is to protect them, so we can present them with an event. It seems to me that if you know the storyline beforehand, the fun is lost."

Nimoy felt that he could *not* make these films by committee. He wouldn't be in a situation which essentially requires that he distribute a questionnaire among the fans and solicit their suggestions. The job had to be left in the hands of the people who have been assigned to it. He felt that while he wasn't entirely insensitive to the concern of the fans, he wouldn't allow himself to be dictated to like an amateur.

Central to the success of the film, as far as Nimoy was concerned, was the input of *Star Trek's* creator:""There was a constant flow of communication from Gene [Roddenberry]. Each draft of the story and script went to him. He responded with very constructive feedback. We discussed his ideas and his reactions to the script. Gene even watched the dailies with me. He was very supportive. His most frequent comment was that the characters were vividly coming to life. He was so delighted with the results, that I felt we must be on the right track." [*Starlog*, July 1984]

At Leonard Nimoy's behest, screenwriter Harve Bennett altered the villains of the script for the new movie, from Romulans to Klingons. Nimoy recalled Bennett's feelings about the script thusly: "Harve [Bennett] wanted to write it, and he seemed capable of doing it, so I felt he should be given that opportunity. [He] captured the sense of *Star Trek* very quickly. He has a strong feeling for the characters.

"We had a good relationship in terms of exchanging ideas. He was extremely responsive to all my suggestions. But I didn't want credit or money for that work. I figured taking on directing would be enough."

As far as the Romulan/Klingon question, Bennett was open to suggestion, as he told *Starlog* in 1986. "I had written the *Star Trek III* script for Romulans, but Leonard felt that the Klingons were more exciting, more theatrical. I went back to some TV episodes, and I realized that he was quite right. A sampling of mail also indicated that the fans wanted to see Klingons. So I rewrote my script and Klingonicized the characters. But I didn't change their ship, because I remembered a piece of trivia that stated there was a mutual assistance military pact between the Klingons and the Romulans for an exchange of military equipment.

"With the Genesis device, we had crippled ourselves in terms of storytelling. In future *Star Treks*, it could have been used as an all-powerful saving device, or the ultimate negative force, the H-bomb of the twenty-fourth century. Something operated in my mind, from *The Man In The White Suit*, a lovely science-fantasy film. Its theme is that for every great advance, you pay a price. Putting protomatter into the hands of David Marcus had created an impossible situation, and then, suddenly, were dealing with guilt."

Bennett realized that he'd painted himself into a corner; dramatic unity called for the death of a character: "So, we wrestled with that decision and, frankly, there were times when we were behaving like the Klingon in the film, passing the knife over Saavik. The one person we couldn't eliminate was Spock. So, it went back and forth between David and Saavik, with the exigency of it having to be real. Then, finally, because we felt it was the logical choice, we committed to killing David.

"That interested me. It all snapped together. Kirk changed the computer on the Kobayashi Maru scenario before *Star Trek II*. His son says to him, 'You've cheated.' His father says, 'I changed the rules.' Well, it turns out that the kettle was calling papa black. He says it at a time when he knows he has changed the rules. I confess to being old fashioned. There is in my vision such a thing as ultimate retribution. The reason David dies, structurally, is because he's messed with mother nature. He allowed himself to bend the rules at the wrong time, in the wrong place. He's there on that planet for only that reason. The whole story dates back to David putting protomatter in the matrix. The death of Spock, everything rests on his shoulders if you want to blame him for it," Bennett stated in the March 198*Enterprise Incidents.*

Ultimately, writer/producer Bennett was extremely pleased with his own script for *The Search for Spock*. "[Frankly], I hadn't done a from-scratch original in years and it was great to do it, to flex the muscles. Having written a screenplay is the greatest satisfaction in the world. It is the hardest thing to begin and the greatest thing to have done. It's a high that rivals any other achievement I've ever had." [*Starlog*, February 1986]

In the February 1985 *Enterprise Incidents,* Bennett related the trials and tribulations of whipping the script for *Star Trek III* into shape.

"It would be very easy to say that at the conclusion of *Star Trek II* that all of the things we have done to modify that film's ending to be ambiguous about the death of Spock were carefully designed and that the plot for *Star Trek III* was already in my mind. Not true. All of that, like most decisions I have ever made, are done in a flurry of intuition and sometimes pressure of time. The last weeks of *Star Trek II* were frenetic because of an organized campaign: DON'T KILL SPOCK1 And the studio panicked that this would affect the box office. Nick Meyer was steadfastly going to walk on the picture. He said that we would kill him, so we're going to kill him. Leonard was getting threatening letters. This was a serious thing and I felt that the compromise we had to make, with Nick's blessing (reluctant though that was) was that we made an ambiguity out of the ending by saying, 'There are always possibilities.' We said, 'Who knows with Vulcans?'

"I have said once or twice at a few Star Trek gatherings I have gone to that I have tried always to be fair. I have a great affection for these people even when they're so proprietary that they come over and tell you that you can't do it your way, you have to do it my way. But these people keep that franchise. It is a business. They keep it strong and healthy. They are its lifeblood. So you do not disregard that. To be fair you've got to give clues and those were the clues we dropped. We also shot an insert of Leonard putting his hand and saying 'Remember.' The very close shot of that wasn't Leonard's hand. In this film we redid that shot because Leonard insisted that his own hand be there. Then I sent a crew to Golden Gate Park (which is Genesis) in San Francisco and we shot the casket. By doing so we said, unbeknownst to them it has soft-landed. I think that was the right series of compromises. We said Spock dies. We do not wish to compromise the impact of that, but this is science fiction and there are always possibilities."

Harve Bennett went on to state, "Somewhere along the line I read a fan poem in one of the hundreds of fan magazines about Star Trek. It was first person Kirk. It said, 'I left you there. Why did I do that? I must come back to you, my friend.' I thought, that's it! I suddenly had a thrust. It got a lot easier from that point. The last scene of this picture is the first scene that I wrote. I don't know if that is unusual but that's the way it was. I wrote it after I read the poem. And later I figured out what scene it was. A great motion picture has a very similar last scene. It was almost, beat for beat, the last scene in *The Miracle Worker* by William Gibson. It is the moment in which, after the entire play, little Helen Keller is at the well with her teacher and she begins to get some understanding, and finally with her hand on her face she says, 'Water,' and the teacher says, 'Yes!' "

Bennett reportedly wrote twelve outlines while working out the various ways to approach the plot, and in spite of being security conscious, one of the outlines got out, was copied and began to be sold by mail and at conventions. Although Bennett claimed to have heard it selling for as high as fifty dollars, I saw it available for no more than ten dollars, which is still pretty high for something twenty pages long.

"At the time it was spooky. How would you like to do what you consider to be a work of art while someone is looking over your shoulder? How would you like to make love while someone else is taking notes and saying, 'It's done this way?' It was very damaging because immediately we feared we'd have another campaign on our hands. Don't kill the Enterprise! Surprisingly, that did not happen. Because the rest of the outline was so man, and so wild, people kind of relaxed about it. So when you're writing with the sense that they're all around you, it's added pressure."

Gene Roddenberry reportedly was against destroying the Enterprise, feeling that it was just a gimmick which was being done to try to outdo the death of Spock. Majel Barrett said as much at convention appearances, confirming in the process that the *Star Trek III* story outline which was circulating among the fans was indeed real. At the time, big name fan Bjo Trimble disbelieved that the outline was real and accused Majel Barrett of " just being mischievous." Bjo insisted that the outline was a forgery "written by a talented fan," as she explained it to me at the time.

But the outline was indeed real, as Bennett confirms, and the following synopsis shows how the story was being developed in its earliest stages.

The story opens with a Romulan ship coming across the Genesis planet and beaming a party down to explore this strange, uncharted world. They immediately discover that the planet contains vast amounts of raw dilithium, the substance used to power the warp engines of starships. The Romulans also find a strange sarcophagus lying on the ground, but upon opening it they find it empty.

The regular Trek characters are seen as the Enterprise returns to Earth. Kirk has not had any response from Starfleet on his handling of the Genesis matter and McCoy is blaming himself for Spock's death. On top of this, people are starting to have visions, what they call visitations, from Spock, and are convinced that he's alive. These are not unlike the visions people had of Kirk in "The Tholian Web" when he was lost in the gateway to another dimension. McCoy even sees Spock in a mirror, just as Uhura saw Kirk in that third season *Star Trek* TV episode.

McCoy's depression grows worse and he requests a leave of absence on Vulcan to try to sort things out for himself. On Vulcan, Kirk and the landing party are attacked and only the appearance of Sarek (Spock's father) halts the conflict. This is where the first major plot problem in the story arises.

It seems that many young Vulcans will not accept their fate being in the hands of the "intellectually inferior Federation" due to the revelation of the power of the Genesis device. This, coupled with Spock's death, is too much for them to handle. But this doesn't work for a number of reasons.

First, how would they even know about the Genesis device? It was blown apart in a remote section of the galaxy and was highly classified. Surely Starfleet would have kept a tight lid on what really happened to the Reliant and Khan, revealing only that Spock had died in a battle with the renegade. The Federation already knew that the Genesis Device could be used as an all-powerful weapon of war, but had decided not to employ it in this manner. It's much more than highly unlikely that the Vulcans would know all about it.

On top of this we have Vulcans reverting to savagery, a concept which is ingrained in them from childhood as being in the worst possible taste. Even the indignities of pon farr are kept within the family and away from all view and knowledge of outsiders.

One interesting point which does arise here is Sarek's resentment that the body of his son was not returned to Vulcan, since he believes the possibility exists that Spock might be alive. He is, after all, an alien with non-human physiology. Upon being confronted with this possibility, and realizing what he has done, Kirk vows to find Spock's body and return it to Sarek.

McCoy elects to remain behind and discover what information Spock left in his mind. This plot thread is also left dangling in the outline, which makes one wonder about the scene during the climax of *Wrath of Khan* when Spock touches McCoy's head with the familiar Vulcan mind meld and says, "Remember," which is not unlike another 1982 release, *E.T.*, wherein at the climax the alien touches Elliott and says, "I'll be right here." Both scenes tend to carry the same implication of stay tuned for the sequel (and even though a sequel to *E.T.* was not consciously planned and has since been discarded entirely, late in the production of that film, Spielberg was still considering calling the movie *E.T. the Extra-Terrestrial, and his First Adventure On Earth*).

In the case of *Wrath Of Khan* a sequel was always planned and everyone felt there was some genuine significance to the Spock/McCoy mind meld. Maybe Harve Bennett just overlooked exploring that avenue in this particular outline, leaving it to be included in a subsequent draft. After all, he said he wrote fourteen outlines before they were satisfied with the plot that they'd worked out.

Back on Genesis, the Romulan vessel destroys a Federation reconnaissance cruiser. So far their mining work on the planet is proceeding undetected.

At Starfleet, Kirk is in hot water for disobeying a direct order and stopping off at Vulcan. He's also in trouble because the Genesis Device was detonated and its existence has triggered intergalactic panic. Now the Romulans and Klingons want parity of Genesis Devices. But hold on now! How could they even know about the Genesis Device? This is top secret stuff, something which above all else the Federation would keep secret under the death penalty, not unlike General Order 7 regarding planet Talos IV. One would also expect that the Guardian planet with its time travel mechanism would also be kept secret in the same manner. So there's just no way that knowledge of the Genesis Device would leak out on such an intergalactic scale. It's not logical. Spies and advanced espionage techniques might detect something, but not enough pieces to assemble into the resolution of the puzzle. So all of the plot elements regarding this widespread knowledge of Genesis just don't wash.

Anyway, back at Starfleet, Kirk's request to return to the Genesis planet meets with a cold response, especially when he leaps up and says, "Now you'll understand—see him there!" because he sees Spock right there in the office of Starfleet. The trouble is, no one else does.

Kirk is reassigned and all the Enterprise personnel are scattered to other ships and duties. Alone in his room, Kirk sees Spock again, but the image fails to answer his entreaties for explanations.

One interesting facet of the story involves Sulu helping Kirk escape from the guard on his room. The rest of the inner circle of the Enterprise crew all conspire and succeed in helping Kirk steal the Enterprise. When the Excelsior, the latest in starships, capable of warp 15 (not transwarp as in the movie), tries to pursue the Enterprise, the Excelsior breaks down because Scotty had been assigned to it before escaping and he'd sabotaged the engines. Nothing like a little mutiny to spice up a plot!

The rest of the story is pretty simple. They reach the Genesis planet and are attacked by the Romulans. The crew evacuates the Enterprise as a large contingent of Romulans beam aboard. Once on the ground, they see the Enterprise explode into tiny pieces, wiping out most of the Romulans.

One interesting idea in all of this was that the Genesis planet was showing signs of volcanic activity and stress, which makes sense because the planet was created out of the stuff of the Mutara Nebula. The Genesis Device was never intended to do any such thing, just to terraform existing planets. When the film threw in this stuff about Genesis being unstable due to protomatter in the matrix, it was unnecessary and ignored the obvious.

In this early story treatment, a new element of mystery emerges as someone (or some thing) is killing off the Romulan sentries one by one and has been there since before the Enterprise returned.

The stalker turns out to be a bearded, amnesiac Spock, who is subdued and beamed aboard the Romulan ship with the rest of the Enterprise party. They find the Romulan vessel practically deserted and capture a female Romulan subcommander. There's a funny line in the treatment which reads: The Bird of Prey roars to life and streaks away from the Genesis planet, which is, with ILM's help, going to implode itself into a black hole.

Their ship then surrenders to a Federation ship and Spock comes around—his old self again. Kirk plans to plead *nolo contendre* to the charges against him, which is the only hint as to the direction Bennett may have been thinking of for *Star Trek IV.*

A story treatment is an idea written up in synopsis form. When one of these is accepted it is used as the blueprint for writing the first draft script. While it's going into script form, many changes are made. Those changes are often major ones as can be seen from comparing this plot to the finished motion picture. Romulans became Klingons, at Leonard Nimoy's request. He liked Klingons better. Genesis was still a secret, one for which there were penalties for anyone who discussed it (which makes more sense than the earlier idea). The rampaging Vulcans idea was lost. The visions of Spock appearing to people were tossed out. The ending was revised, although it still achieved the same purpose. What was retained is as striking as what was not. The treatment is an interesting examination of the Genesis planet and the transformation of ideas as they were developed and worked with by other hands. For instance, David Marcus was not killed in the early story treatment.

It still seems that the Enterprise was cast aside just to get an explosive special effect. It certainly wasn't something that Gene Roddenberry wanted to see happen. But Bennett denied this. In the December 1984 issue of *Enterprise Incidents,* the writer/producer stated, "There was no exterior—that is to say, no non-story—reason for the destruction of the Enterprise. The logic of the story compelled the moves. We did not start with any clear idea that the Enterprise was doomed."

Since Gene Roddenberry opposed the destruction of the starship, he and Bennett discussed alternatives, such as allowing part of the Enterprise to be saved by having a saucer separation and then using it in a clever way later in the story. But Bennett opposed this idea, feeling that this, "vitiated the decision Kirk had to make." He felt this would cheat the audience since Kirk would be sacrificing the starship at the price of his own survival.

There were other considerations facing Bennett in *Star Trek III*, as it became apparent that they would need to re-cast the role of Lieutenant Saavik. Kirstie Alley, apparently, wanted a considerably larger salary than that which she'd received for *The Wrath of Khan.*

"Our big problem came with the lady who played Saavik," Bennett explained in the March 1985 issue of *Enterprise Incidents*. "She wanted as much as Bill Shatner. We thought it was funny at first. There was no movement in negotiation. We thought that Saavik's part in this was wonderful. We didn't want to cut it out." So they decided to re-cast the character and keep the part. "How did we fare in putting Robin Curtis in where Kirstie Alley had gone before? About even. Curiously enough, no one has said a thing. Part of it is probably that Alley had a different quality. The character's latent sexuality was very appealing and indicated that there was something under that that might be Romulan. Robin is almost pure Vulcan. She too falls into this stylistic category. And Leonard directing was much more inclined to Vulcanize her rather than dig for the Romulan."

In fact, Robin Curtis brought a completely new approach to the character, unencumbered by any prior notions or conceits, as the actress explained: "I have no idea who Saavik was because I didn't see *Star Trek II* or even *Star Trek: The Motion Picture,*" she admitted candidly. "I still haven't though I would like to now. So I came to it objectively."

"I didn't have any hunger for a science-fiction angle, just from an actress' point-of-view. I didn't have as much at stake as someone who was aware of the role and would give their eye teeth to do it. So, maybe I gave off a cool, clear-headed attitude. The slate was clean for me. No one had to fight with anything I had already drawn in my head as to what a Vulcan or Romulan was. I had no prior stereotypes." [*Starlog*, June 1984]

Robin Curtis was born in Utica, New York, and was actively involved in music and in performing from an early age. She began acting while a student at the State University of New York at Oswego, NY, and took part in many musical productions. In 1978 she relocated to New York City, where she landed small stage roles and worked occasionally on soap operas. Commercial work soon seemed to be her main source of income, although she had a small role in the movie *Ghost Story*. A move to Los Angeles led to a TV movie, a role on *Knight Rider* (that's called "paying your dues") and ultimately to her casting interview with Leonard Nimoy.

Her lack of preconceptions was anything but a hindrance, as Nimoy was all-too-willing to give her a crash-course in the finer points of being a Vulcan. He explained to her that there are thousands of years of wisdom right behind their eyes. Curtis tried to project that idea. Nimoy told her a story about the first TV episode of *Star Trek*. . . Leonard was still trying to find the key to his role. Spock was supposed to say, 'Fascinating.' And he did. The director came over and said, 'No, Leonard. You're different from everyone else here. You should be reacting as a scientist. It's not FASCINATING, it's fascinating.' That was the birth of the cool reaction.

Of course, Robin Curtis was cast as a character originally essayed by another actress, and there was a possibility, for a while, that Kirstie Alley might return. "My manager knew that things weren't working out with Kirstie [Alley]. But I don't think they would have started looking for another Saavik if there was much chance of her coming back. [I] didn't feel bad about the situation because I knew she was doing *Cat On A Hot Tin Roof* on stage.

I don't want to think my good fortune came at the expense of someone else's misfortune. I've never met Kirstie or spoken to her, so I don't know the casting situation forehand." Fortunately, Kirstie Alley was about to break through to stardom when she joined the cast of the hit situation comedy *Cheers*— and pulled off the seemingly impossible task of replacing Shelley Long.

This was good news, not only for Robin Curtis, but for another member of her family as well. "[My older brother] got thrilled when I got the role. He wrote me a funny letter in Vulcanese, saying, "It is logical that you should be a movie star." It had a stardate and everything. Then he immediately put in a request for badges."

With such congratulations out of the way, it was down to work for the *Star Trek* crew and its latest member. "A great deal has to do with the look, and right from the first interview, Leonard was watching my expression and scrutinizing me," recalled Curtis. "I have very curly hair. They didn't want a contemporary look, but something more sleek with straight lines. So, I was fitted with a hairpiece. My hair in front was blown straight back; the piece came straight down in the back. I looked like Princess Caroline. Fortunately, they didn't like it either, and we went back to my own hair. They wanted a softer look. My hair was just trimmed so that the ears were exposed."

"Kirstie's eyebrows weren't done at all. Leonard asked me if I was willing to shave mine. I said, "I want to look as true to a Vulcan as I can." I might even have shaved my head if that's what Leonard wanted. I felt the eyebrows were a must, not just because it would be authentic, but because such changes help an actress. In those three hours in the makeup chair every morning, you become transformed."

The first two weeks on the set Curtis worried up to the first day she would have to speak a word in front of the camera. She spent a few days in the background first, to get to know everybody. She had nightmares that she would appear on the set naked or forget her lines—typical actor nightmares. But after that first day ended, she was so energized she wanted to say, 'Can't we do it again?'

"I constantly battled with not revealing emotions. I had to guard against even the slightest hint of emotion. When Saavik is witty, it was hard for me not to be sarcastic. Leonard kept saying, 'Dry. Dry. Drier.'"

"In this movie, Saavik shows she has a heart and compassion. She cares. But she's also a very good Vulcan." [*Starlog*, June 1984]

In addition to the destruction of the Enterprise, *Star Trek III* featured the demise of Kirk's son David, who redeems his previous folly by getting himself killed instead of Saavik. But this plot wrinkle meant that another character couldn't be on hand, lest she complicate a delicate situation. Thus Carol Marcus, David's mother, is nowhere to be scene before, during or after her son's death.

As Bennett explained in *Enterprise Incidents*, "She was the fifth member of a four man relay team. She was the extraneous character. She was in the story outline. I thought it might be fun to have her relating to David and have something going with Saavik. But then protomatter came up. Then something happened: Did Carol know? If Carol knows about protomatter, everything about David making a mistake—cheating, being responsible—doesn't wash. Then it's not David's ambition, it's mother and son in some kind of Oedipal whim to cheat the world together, and they don't tell Kirk, which is very out of character. Also, then I would have had to kill them both. Writer's problem. Answer: Don't get Carol involved. Get her out of this issue. David doing it without his mother's knowledge enriches it for me, and his father certainly doesn't know.

"If you think it's tough answering that, think of how it was when I tried to explain it to Bibi Besch. She was deeply upset. She cried. She thought it was a rejection of her talent. Now I've said enough about actors. Bibi's a very adult actress, so you can understand that that may sound strange to you, but it is not. She thought she must have done something wrong. But I got a lovely letter from Bibi after the picture opened. It said, 'I've seen the picture. Now I understand. You were right. I hope you can find a place for me in one of the other films.' " Although the character of Carol Marcus has not appeared in any of the subsequent films, she does occupy an important place in the Vonda McIntyre novelization of *Star Trek III: The Search For Spock*. The book has considerably more plot than the film, and Carol Marcus is shown returning to Earth to meet with the families of her assistants who had been slain by Khan in *Star Trek II*. The book even relates those experiences, making for a considerably more complex narrative than the motion picture provides. All of that additional material was conceived by Vonda McIntyre and was not based on anything discarded by Harve Bennett from the screenplay.

Bennett was particularly moved by William Shatner's work in *Star Trek III*. The drama of the script hinged on believing that Captain Kirk would do these extraordinary things and feel this extraordinary grief.

"I'll tell you what was a great directorial achievement by Leonard was getting emotion over David's death out of Shatner because he wanted to play it more stylistically. It's the only scene I remember where Leonard said, 'Clear the bridge.' Literally. He said, 'Will everyone please leave. I want to talk to Bill.' I never asked him what he said to Bill. It was very personal. It was director talk to actors."

Regarding that scene, Nimoy stated, "On the day of shooting that scene, he and I kind of got ourselves off into a corner and discussed it slowly in a relaxed atmosphere, and privately. What I said to him was this. I said, 'You have to decide how far you want to take this reaction. My opinion is that you can go pretty far and get away with it; maybe strip off some of the veneer of the admiral, the hero, always in charge, always on top of the situation, and show us a vulnerable person.' He took it further, frankly, than I expected him to, and it was scary. I mean, how many space epics do you see where your hero, on receiving personal news, stumbles back and falls on the person's own ship? You don't see that a lot. It was a scary thing for all of us hoping that it would be perceived as a very touching moment. Some little kid breaks out in laughter in the audience and you're dead.

"We did several takes and used the one where we really thought Bill lost control and fell. It looked accidental, not a performance. I'm very moved by it. In my opinion it is some of the best work he has ever done. It looked as though he had received a physical jolt, as if somebody had hit him with the information. He looks deeply hurt. Some of the most personal and vulnerable work I've ever seen done in the role of Kirk."

Principal photography for Star Trek III was completed on October 21, 1983. The task of fleshing out the gaps in the film's images went, once more, to George Lucas' Industrial Light and Magic. Nimoy found the people at ILM totally supportive and "wildly imaginative."

ILM production supervisor Warren Franklin revealed, in a 1984 interview in the pages of *Cinefex* magazine, what that entailed for him and his team. "*Star Trek II* was a great project for ILM. We got involved from the very, very beginning. . . myself, Nilo Rodis and David Carson, the two art directors. We started back in November of 1982, when we got the original two-page outline that Harve Bennett had written. It seemed like a real solid, action-packed story, well-constructed and everything. then we got the first script early in 1983, which also read very well. It was one of the best scripts we read— and I must get a script a week from productions that are looking for effects work. We basically executed [the storyboards], adding what we could, but a lot of the [special effects] stuff was already decided."

Nilo Rodis, Ken Ralston and Dave Carson] worked very closely with Leonard Nimoy and Harve Bennett. They did the key illustrations for all the main sets on Genesis, and designed the new *Excelsior* spaceship, the *Bird of Prey*. They also designed the new scout-class vehicle the *Grissom*, and did a new space dock for Earth to replace the one from Star Trek—The Motion Picture.

"In some of the initial meetings," Franklin continued, "Michael Fulmer and some of the other model makers came up with quick little prototypes that helped everyone get a much better idea of what we were talking about. We had four or five space stations that we'd designed, and a couple of *Birds of Prey*. During one meeting, in particular, we had a space station that was getting pretty close, but they wanted a few things changed. So we took it over to Bill George, and half an hour later he came back with the changes. Then we talked about it again and changed it some more. It was kind of a 'visual sketching' that gave them a direction to head for, something to strive for. We wanted to get as much locked down at the beginning as we could, because the sooner we got started, the more time we would have on the work."

Effects photographer Scott Farrar recalled working on the sequence in which the battle-scarred *Enterprise* returns to space dock. "We spent a couple of months just doing space dock interiors. There weren't any complex moves, but they were very time consuming, to get all the various passes and smoke it up and all. We tested a lot of different looks to make the interior of the dock seem appropriately vast. After trying various things, we found that the interior demanded some degree of atmospheric haze, even though there probably wouldn't be any in outer space. It just needed help to look slightly degraded, not so crisp and clean. As a result, we ended up using blue gels on the lights and shooting in smoke for the basic 'fill' look. Then, when we went to the light passes, we used a diffusion filter. We could have used smoke, but because the light passes were so long, we would have to have had a system where our smoke level was constantly controlled. We opted not to do that because we had so many shots."

It wasn't possible to shoot any of the ships actually in the space dock because none of the scales matched. They shot the Enterprise floating out first—they could get away with a lot there, since it was moving. But it was difficult doing the ships that were supposed to remain stationary, relative to the dock wall, while the camera itself was moving. They shot a lot of black-and-white tests— practice shots— trying to lock in with the background. Each shot had to be plotted out on the Movieola, point to point on a grid system. It had to look like the ships were glued to a wall, and even though they can do a lot with calibrations and numbers, they basically had to just keep doing it until it looked right.

"We were on that [dock sequence] for a couple of months. As we completed the background, Don Dow would immediately start plugging in ships. Every once in a while, we'd break out of that to shoot another ship at the other end of the track, because optical would be waiting for one single element, and we wouldn't want to hold them up any longer. Still, it seemed like we were in there for a long time. Almost like a camp-out in your own little room. For weeks."

They had a lot of lights outside the space dock to light all the little pinholes, in addition to the fiber optics everywhere and the little miniature practical lights on the inside. The combination of all those things gave the space dock its 'lit' look from wall to ceiling to floor. But when the doors opened, they would obscure the pinhole lights, so they would have to run fiber optics beneath the doors to the wall that would be otherwise covered up. The trick was always to match the lighting and make sure there weren't any flares going into the lens from all the different angles of the lights. In some cases they had eighteen stage lights running outside and had to have the fans blowing constantly on the outside of the space dock to keep everything cool. Otherwise, it would warp all the artwork on the inside of the wall and destroy it. The doors themselves were supposed to have lit panels inside them, so they required a separate pass of their own. The technicians had a rig that was actually mounted on the door— lights aimed into the boxes built onto the door, so they could get an evenly toned light on the translucent material.

Director Nimoy, with cast and crew, actually travelled to ILM to shoot one scene, the only one shot off the Paramount lot. The scene involved a conversation in the Starfleet dockside cafeteria, with a window looking out upon the seemingly vast space dock as a background to the expository dialogue.

Ken Ralston recalled how it was accomplished: "The cafeteria scene has a live-action foreground that's a set we did here at ILM with about forty extras. On top of that, a matte painting is added to complete the rest of the cafeteria from the inside. Through the window, you see the Enterprise, which is a miniature composited in later, and behind that you see the back side of the space dock. It's a tremendous shot; you get all this scope and scale that doesn't occur most of the time, and we could only do a shot like that because of the very large blue screen we have here at ILM."

Ralston also recalled the considerable length of some of the special effects shots the ILM team had to put together for *Star Trek III*. "They're exceedingly long shots, some of the longest I've ever worked on, where we have four or five hundred frames. Most of the shots in the *Star Wars* films were never over a hundred frames. Many of them were twenty frames long. So you can get away with a lot, especially if something is moving fast. If the matter doesn't fit exactly right, you're not going to see it; it's against the stars, and it's there and gone so quickly that your mind isn't going to detect a big error in it. But in these, everything is lit, you're backed against a light background, and if the matte doesn't fit, you'll see it. It's like Mack Sennett. Just go from one thing to the next, so they won't think. You don't want to keep reminding everyone that what they're seeing is impossible. There's one shot in Trek, a matte painting near the end, that I think they hold on longer than any matte painting ever. It still holds up, but. . . {I was] clawing at the arms of my seat saying, 'It's too long, too long!' "

But even the technicians at Industrial Light & Magic, whose job it was to do the actual blowing up of the ship, had mixed feelings about it. Special Effects Supervisor Ken Ralston had this to say in the November 1984 issue of *Fantastic Films.*

"Personally, I would love to take credit for blowing up the Enterprise—I've been wanting to do it for years! I always thought it would be an incredibly emotional moment if it were done properly. And, of course, if the fans were *really* offended by the loss of the Enterprise, we could always postulate that Starfleet has a huge mothball fleet of similar ships and they could always reactivate another one." Ralston went on to make the observation, "The Enterprise had character. Come to think of it, I don't know if the fans would ever accept any ship other than the Enterprise."

In *Cinefex* #18 (August 1984), Ralston explained how they destroyed the venerable NCC-1701.

"The whole ship blows up in a series of shots. The bridge goes, then the ship starts to keel over and—this is the shot I just *had* to get in—you see the famous NCC-1701 sapping away in a real close shot. Then the saucer comes up towards the camera, and the whole thing blows up in one big, fiery mass. Then there's a long shot of the Enterprise falling out, with most of the dome blown off and only the gridwork left. It falls into the planet and we have a few long shots of this comet going down, seen from the surface as Kirk and his people stand there, and he's saying, 'What have I done?' It's a good moment—very powerful."

For the shots involving the actual destruction of the Enterprise, ILM technician Ted Moehnke and his crew worked with partial models which were quickly destroyed and not any of the actual Enterprise models used in previous films. A new Enterprise model, one-third smaller than what was normally photographed, was built for full shots of the partially destroyed starship. "We had to do this in a way that would be very dramatic," Moehnke said. "We started out with the little dome, and a lot of little explosions with cannons and balloons inside the ship. It's timing that makes it work—timing that gives you rhythm, gives you scale." The final explosion was photographed at 360 frames a second—with explosions timed to within three or four frames.

"The easy thing about building the model," technician Don Dow explained, "was that it didn't have to be that extensive as far as lights and things. The whole bridge area had been blown away, so there were no more lights on the ship. We wanted the skin to melt away prior to the dome blowing up, as if there was an inner heat that caused it to melt. We made a dome that was about six or eight feet in diameter, using a very thin styrene plastic for the shell, and then we shot it at a slow frame rate—a quarter of a second per frame—as we dropped acetone on the surface. Of course, the acetone ate the plastic away, and when that's sped up to 24 frames per second, it really looks like a melting effect. We actually sprayed it on the outside while we were shooting. The problem we had was that we could see the drops on the first test—it looked like rain coming down. So we had to devise different methods of spraying the acetone on; and we used different chemicals, too. Other solvents would react with the plastic at different rates. A couple of places where we had decals for the numbers wouldn't melt as fast as the other areas, so it was a little bit tricky. Then we went in and did the fire effects, shooting again with the same program and the same frame rate."

To get the fire effects, the entire dome was laid over with steel wool which was lit in several areas at once to create burning pools in different areas. This resulted in a deep glow rather than actual flames, thereby creating the illusion of something burning in the vacuum of space.

Actually, the fire is burning the oil that's on the steel wool, and the steel is melting. But as the steel wool burns, a lot of tiny shards fly off; and they drop and create a fireworks effect. They want that, so animation had to go in and rotoscope it all out. They tried to eliminate it as much as possible on the stage by using spray bottles with water to extinguish the embers as they came off the model. But what they found which was even better was just being very careful about how they spread the steel wool. The steel wool comes in a pad and was carefully unrolled to get a flat, smooth piece about six or twelve inches long.

The creatures that populated the Genesis planet were created by David Sosalla, who sculpted the rapidly-evolving worm creatures that pose such a problem to new visitors to Genesis. First came the smaller version. "We made them from Hot-Melt, which is the same material squirmy toys are made from— a material you heat to a certain temperature. We had to try and keep it clear, too— they wanted a translucent feeling to everything, so we had to be careful about the temperature. The Hot-Melt burns easily, and once it burns, it turns brown. [We would go through] the [worm] molds fairly quickly, even though we're not set up for doing large batches of Hot-Melt. After we had a hundred or more of these things, we painted them using a lot of methacyl, which is a real slimy goo.

"[Then we] ran fishlines all around [the set], and through a bunch of holes. [The worms were attached to the fishline.] We tied them to rods underneath, and made some other little rods that would come up and poke at the worms. The idea was to have enough undulation to make them look alive and to avoid dead spots. We would have as many as ten or fifteen people under there pushing these rods up and down, pulling on fishline so they'd go 'squish squish.' "

Unfortunately, these critters were obliged to evolve into larger, uglier monster worms, which give Klingon Commander Kruge (Christopher Lloyd) a bit of a tussle as he's investigating this strange new world. David Sosalla remembered them vividly, if not exactly fondly. "They're a bit like the Ceti eels from Star Trek II. It was necessary to give some kind of motion to the front of them, to make them look meaner than just a wormy head. . . I came up with a system [of making the worms move] of making these long preshaped air bladders that I'd hook up to a series of quick-connect air hoses. Then I could pile these things, have several switches for the air passages, and two people could push these little switches. one set of bags would fill and move into their predesignated shapes. Then you'd let the air out of those, and inject air into another set of bags, and other worms would undulate. They gave a real organic movement to the worms. . . And we'd have people off to the side pulling tail-end pieces through the shot, so that there would be some additional crawling and undulation. The visualization of the movement was exciting when you could stand back and play with it, but the final cut is so quick you never get the full impact." [*Cinefex*, Aug. 1984]

When the worms attacked Commander Kruge, Sosalla and crew had a problem on their hands. There was so much slime on the worms that it would have shown in the shot when they reversed it. They couldn't do a lot of takes because it would have ruined Kruge's makeup. So, it was filmed in real time. One cut shows a worm wrapping around Kruge's arm. For that, all they had to do was have the string attached to the worm going around Kruge's arm. Then two people in front would use their lines to pass it over. The lucky fellow getting attacked by these charming creatures, Commander Kruge, was portrayed by Christopher Lloyd, fresh from his tenure as "Reverend" Jim on the television series *Taxi*. Jim, of course, was a Trekkie (and would probably be offended by the term "trekker") who wore an *E.T.* button on his faded denim jacket throughout a great many episodes of that comedy classic; it was only fitting that his alter-ego, Christopher Lloyd, should have a chance to actually be in a *Star Trek* movie. Lloyd certainly enjoyed playing a heavy, worms or no worms, as he told in a fan magazine interview:

"Villains are often a little more extravagant in their behavior and give you different things to do that a straight character doesn't always allow you to do. They're a little more theatrical and a little more fun to play with ."

"The costume and make-up, if nothing else, certainly set a tone for me and I just tried to fill it in. I liked the character make-up, and with the costume combined, it really gave, in my mind, an image of the character that was fun to play with. The costume made me look regal, which I felt Kruge was. When I would put the costume on, immediately I would stand a certain way and walk a certain way. It forced me to take a posture that made me feel good for the character. It helped me become the character even more when I would see myself in the make-up and the costume."

"The Klingon language was kind of difficult because it doesn't relate to anything but itself. It's just a series of different kinds of sounds that have been designated as actual words with meanings. It's just difficult to memorize them and then try to put it all together and make it sound like real speech." [*ST:TOFCM* #47]

Christopher Lloyd has had a long association with fantasy and science-fiction genre films, having appeared in *The Adventures of Buckaroo Banzai*, all three *Back To The Future* films, and the recent smash hit *The Addams Family*, where he portrays Uncle Fester. Other films include Nicholas Roeg's *Track 29, The Onion Field, Goin' South*, and *One Flew Over The Cuckoo's Nest*, which was his film debut.

While not the monumental villain that Ricardo Montalban was as Khan, Lloyd creates a worthy adversary in the imperious Kruge.

But Kruge was not the only threat in *Star Trek III*; the Genesis planet itself was a hellishly dangerous place. The entire film is highly dramatic, of course, hinging as it does on the recovery of a lost friend. Although Nimoy found directing a motion picture quite a challenge, he surrounded himself with very capable technical personnel.

When released in 1984 opposite *Ghostbusters* and *Indiana Jones And The Temple of Doom,* the motion picture was nevertheless just as successful as *The Wrath of Khan* and served as the plum in Nimoy's resume which enabled him to step in and take over on the Touchstone film *Three Men And a Baby,* which would turn out to be an even bigger hit than *Star Trek III.*

Among the reviews *Star Trek III* received was a glowing one by Richard Schickel in the June 11, 1984 issue of *Time* which included the following observation: "The result is perhaps the first space opera to deserve that term in its grandest sense. The plot is as convoluted and improbable as anything Verdi ever set to music; the settings are positively Wagnerian in scale and, especially at the climax, full of his kind of fiery mysticism. Above all, the emotions of *Star Trek III* are as broad and as basic as anything this side of Rigoletto. Principally, these are the province of Admiral James T Kirk (William Shatner, of course). His attempt to answer the cries for help that Spock transmits by means of a mysterious Vulcanic technique known as a 'mindmeld' forces him to the most anguishing command decisions. These involve the life and death of his son and the fate of his beloved starship Enterprise."

One of the more interesting comments on *Star Trek III* was made by Nicholas Meyer in the December 1991 *Cinefantastique*. Meyer had bitterly fought Harve Bennett against the last minute change in the ending of *Star Trek II: The Wrath of Khan* which made Spock's death seem more ambiguous than it had originally been written.

"I wasn't considering what they were doing as immoral, just aesthetically misled. I don't believe you can bring a dead person back to life. Having seen it in *Star Trek III,* I still don't believe it. But okay, he's back, Leonard is back, and since it's Leonard, I'm happy."

Leonard Nimoy was not on Paramount's hit parade. However, feeling up to the task ahead, Nimoy made the unprecedented move of agreeing to direct a second Star Trek film, making him the first director to helm more than one of the feature film projects.

FOUR: THE VOYAGE HOME

"This is easily the most absurd of the Star Trek stories and yet, oddly enough,, it is also the best, the funniest and the most enjoyable in simple human terms." —Roger Ebert, New York Post

Star Trek IV: The Voyage Home entered production with high hopes all around. *The Search for Spock* had been a great success, with profits (and costs) roughly equal to those of the second film, proving to Paramount that they had, after all, a viable commercial property in the form of an on-going *Star Trek* film series. A fourth film was a certainty, and Paramount, hoping for a replay, once again turned to Leonard Nimoy to direct.

Star Trek IV: The Voyage Home was the most successful film in the series to date.

The tone of this film was considerably different from its predecessors. Early in the writing process, Harve Bennett decided that this was an important consideration:

"This movie will be more lighthearted. Our audience deserves it. I think that if we were still doing a TV series, every third show would tend to be: 'Let's lighten up, folks.' " [*Starlog*, February 1986]

"[Both] Leonard and I, in the beginning, felt that we had to lighten up from all the life-and-death situations we had in the previous motion pictures. That was not only for story purposes but because all of us felt we needed to breathe. Most of my choices in material for the *Star Trek* films that I have done have been heavily influenced by the initial two months when I saw all the episodes for the first time. I began to make my own list of the things I had loved and the things I had not cared about and began to make my own list of top ten. I was shocked to find that my top ten closely coincided with the fans' top ten and the highest selling cassettes. I had obviously come through the same experience the fans had.

"I didn't set out to do a trilogy. Events created that. You know, the pursuit of Leonard, the turnaround when they found out we were going to kill Spock, so we had to rewrite to make sure if we were going to kill him we would have to do it climactically. Once we brought him back, we left him there with an empty head. So throughout those films, I knew we were going to have to deal with all those problems. I also knew that the second most popular episode and cassette over the years was 'The City On The Edge Of Forever.' Early on, I said, 'We have to do time travel.'

"San Francisco has always been *Star Trek* headquarters. It has been the headquarters of Starfleet, not only in our movies, but in the TV series.

Storywise, you could say, 'Let's go back in time to Australia,' but obviously for unity of tale, you know you're going to have to go back to the place you left. Since the place you left is Starfleet headquarters, you don't want them saving the world by returning to Brisbane, Australia and then getting on the phone and saying, 'Hello, we've just saved the world down here.' "

[*ST:TOFCM* #55]

Director-to-be Leonard Nimoy was concerned that the crisis in the film not be too heavy, and pondered what sort of dilemma the Enterprise crew should face. "We didn't want to make a movie about people dying of diseases all over the place," Nimoy noted in a 1987 *Cinefantastique* question-and-answer session, recalling early notions that had the Enterprise crew seeking something— a medicinal plant, perhaps— needed to save the world from an unbeatable disease. "That didn't seem very appealing. It also didn't seem to be very appealing to be flying through space with a plant. Then, one night, I was talking to a friend of mine about endangered species and up came the subject of the humpback whales and the mysterious song they sing. We don't know exactly what it is or what it means. I thought, 'That's it!' If we can pull that off, sending humpback whales three hundred years through space, that would be exciting. And that's how the story evolved."

Harve Bennett was quite receptive to Nimoy's new idea. "We knew this much: they had to come back for something which was lost in the Twenty-third Century and which was needed to save it. That was the premise. We talked about oil refining and how that would be a lost art in the Twenty-third Century and about nuclear energy and all kinds of things they would have to come back to the Twentieth Century for. Then one day, Leonard came in. [and] he said, 'What would you think if we used whales?' And I said, 'You're asking your producer if he wants to make a movie about whales? And not only whales, but humpbacks, who are not trainable?' He said, 'Well, that's true, but I don't think Orcas will do it.' And I said, 'Well, Orcas have already been done and it would be silly because they are sort of giant lovables now even though they're called killer whales.

There have been five movies on killer whales. . . if we do whales, it's got to be either great blues or humpbacks.' Then we found out that only humpbacks sing, great blues don't. From that point on, it was only a question of whether we could bring the idea to life. But the idea Leonard came up with was so outstanding and so noble that we couldn't look elsewhere after that no matter what our fears were about pulling it off. So we started out with the time travel element and then combined it with the story about whales."

[ST:TOFCM #55]

An initial script draft was completed in August 1985 by the writing team of Steve Meerson and Peter Krikes. Another factor loomed as well: Paramount Picture's biggest box office draw, comedy superstar Eddie Murphy, appeared to be keenly interested in being in the film. Rumors abounded; many feared, and perhaps rightly, that Murphy would dominate the movie at the expense of the regular characters. Still, a role was written with him in mind, though it could have, in a pinch, been played by anyone. Eventually, Murphy's attention turned elsewhere.

Bennett went through every writer they could think of and finally found Steve Meerson and Peter Krikes, whose work was highly regarded by the studio. Nothing came of it. Some of that, in fairness to them, was because Bennett and company had saddled them with what appeared to be a male character that they thought was going to be Eddie Murphy. Then when Eddie Murphy fell out, they had to readjust the script. But by then Bennett no longer felt that the script was working. Bennett claimed that there were only two scenes in the picture that they wrote that stayed pretty much the same. One of them is the hospital scene that had minor modifications by Nick Meyer and Harve Bennett. Meerson and Krikes had also laid down the outline for the Plexiglass factory scene. But at that point, Bennett didn't have a script he felt good about or that he could even submit to the studio. Krikes and Meerson had slightly different recollections of these events.

In describing their experiences writing the early version of the screenplay, Krikes explained, "Steve and I worked closely with Leonard and Harve to outline the story."

"And when the studio approved it, we wrote the script," stated Meerson during a lunchtime interview at the Paramount commissary in 1986. "So during those first months when we were hired, it was just a battery of meetings between Leonard, Harve, Peter and myself so that we could get the story into shape to write the screenplay."

The writers state that they were well aware that a lot of Trek fans were angry over the announced possibility of having Eddie Murphy in the film. Fans remembered all too well the way comedian Richard Pryor was used to the detriment of *Superman III*. But Krikes and Meerson rejected that parallel.

"That's not anything like what we did," Krikes insisted. "*Superman III* was a very bad script." Although written with Eddie Murphy in mind, the character they were writing would have have been just another version of the comedian's familiar screen persona.

"He was a 20th century human who becomes aware of these visitors from the future. It wasn't written specifically for Murphy—Robin Williams could have played him."

But as to whether their screenplay had been a comedy, the writing team agreed that they wouldn't term it such, exactly.

"I wouldn't call it a comedy, but it's the funniest one of the four—excluding the first one," Krikes observed dryly. "It's like the episodes they used to have of the TV series which were humorous. It has some exciting moments. The ending is terrific. You really do have a rooting interest for these people."

"It's like an old-fashioned movie where you feel very good when you walk out of it," said Meerson, underscoring what his writing partner had to say. "It has a different look than any of the other *Star Trek's* and a little bit of a different approach." So while he agreed that there are humorous moments, he explained that the humor definitely comes out of the situations.

While Harve Bennett, as producer of *Star Trek IV,* was involved with the project from the beginning, he initially was only co-plotting rather than writing. When Steve Meerson and Peter Krikes turned in their completed script, the planned start date for principal photography was only several weeks away.

"What was happening," said Krikes, "was that they were in a rush. They felt that they needed the script so that they could start shooting in October [1985]. Since Harve was much more familiar with *Star Trek* than we were, he felt that he could do what was needed much quicker than we could."

"We believe that he could have," Meerson agreed, "since he had done these things before. They're not easy to write. On the surface they may appear to be easy, but they're really not. They're probably the hardest scripts to write that I've ever done, and when it came time to put in those nuances, I really thought it was time for the guy who had done them before to step in and do it."

When told that it had been rumored that Bennett had been unhappy with the screenplay the duo turned in, Krikes expressed surprise and stated, "Harve's always been nice to us and he's never said anything bad about us that we know of."

"Peter and I are still working at Paramount," Meerson pointed out during the 1986 interview. "We like it here and we had a very nice time with those people working on that project."

"We worked very closely with Leonard Nimoy on this," Krikes stated. "He is truly a gentleman and was a lot of fun," Meerson added.

At the time they were unaware that Bennett had brought in Nicholas Meyer to work on the rewrite with him. When the script for *Star Trek IV* went to the Writer's Guild for ar-

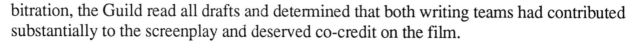

bitration, the Guild read all drafts and determined that both writing teams had contributed substantially to the screenplay and deserved co-credit on the film.

In describing things they contributed to the storyline, they focus on the way the supporting players are used in the story. For instance, it was their idea to bring Dr. Chapel back into the series for her first appearance since *Star Trek: The Motion Picture*. They also thought it was quite important that Amanda be there because of what happened to Spock in the third film. Krikes and Meerson didn't feel that the other characters got enough to do in the old series, and so they tried to give them all something to do in this movie. They all have different tasks that they have to accomplish separately where you get to see them away from Kirk and Spock.

Although the *Star Trek IV* script was rewritten by producer Harve Bennett and Nicholas Meyer, it remained the basic idea first conceived by Bennett and Nimoy. The rough equivalent of the Eddie Murphy role became that of Dr. Gillian Taylor (Catherine Hicks), the focal Twentieth Century character.

Catherine Hicks, a native of New York City, grew up in Scottsdale, Arizona. She majored in English Literature before going on to Cornell University, where she concentrated on acting. After graduation, she returned to New York and landed a part on *Ryan's Hope*.

More television work followed: the title role in *Marilyn: The Untold Story* garnered her an Emmy nomination and great visibility. Such series as *Tucker's Witch* and *Valley of the Dolls*, although all but forgotten now, also found a place for her talents. After her film debut in the Bill Murray remake of Somerset Maugham's *The Razor's Edge*, Hicks was involved in Sidney Lumet's *Garbo Talks* and in Frances Ford Coppola's *Peggy Sue Got Married*. From there it was a short leap to her pivotal role in *Star Trek IV: The Voyage Home*. But Catherine Hicks was new to *Star Trek* in more ways than one.

"I was on the other channel in childhood," she admits. "I'm not really proud of it because when I got to college, the smarter people had been Trekkies. But I believe it worked to my advantage because I wasn't intimidated by them. After we stopped shooting I watched all the shows and, frankly, I would have been intimidated. I sort of have a crush on Spock, now. When I did the picture it was, 'Hi, Leonard, how're you doing?' and it was no big deal. Even after I got the role, I decided since Gillian doesn't know what's going on, maybe I should just use my ignorance to my advantage."

Still, Hicks had a difficult time landing the role. "I'd thought, well, this won't be too hard, but Leonard was really specific in what he wanted. I was greatly humbled. I had to come back four times; it was a very long process. I really had to prove myself. I had to be spunky but intelligent. The first audition was a knockout—Leonard loved it, but the video cameras broke. I had to come back and I was off, so he knew it wasn't that great and that made him nervous again. And then they had to come back and we had to go to an old horse ranch to meet Bill and his horse, and I was real nervous. I thought, 'God, if the horse doesn't like me they'll think I'm not good with animals.' I was like, 'Hi, horse!' I'm cool with animals, and finally Leonard took me aside and I'll never forget the feeling when he just said, 'Welcome to *Star Trek*.' Those moments make all the hardships of being an actor worthwhile."

In preparing for the role of Gillian Taylor, she visited Sea World and did a few interviews with marine biologists. She talked to people about marine biologists and watched a National Geographic special about a woman who worked with a whale at Sea World. When it had to be released, she was very upset. She was a scientist but everybody at this place got very attached to these creatures. They loved them and they got love in return. The special had one shot at the end where, after they're about to go home, there's a silhouette of this woman sitting on the edge as the sun sets—she's lost her best friend. Hicks felt that seeing that helped give her a lot of insight into her character.

Regarding how it was to work with director Nimoy, Hicks stated, "His perception was so very helpful. He knew how to get you out of a tough spot and keep away from pitfalls. But he really didn't want me to be too much into the whales because he thought that would be kinky. If I had it to do over again, I would have lightened up a bit. The only thing is, I've been told that people in that profession are very protective; that it's almost a maternal thing.

Leonard Nimoy as a director is really calm, and as you can see, I need that. It helped me. He's just that way by nature. I don't know whether he worked through it in the sixties, like some people did, or whether it's his nature. He's just very calm. He set the tone for the set. He just helped everyone relax and feel confident. You knew he was in charge and you knew what he wanted."

Star Trek IV also promised to feature the largest number of *Star Trek* alumni in any of the motion pictures; not only did Dr. Chapel, now a Commander (Majel Barrett) and Commander Janice Rand (Grace Lee Whitney) make their first appearances since *Star Trek: The Motion Picture*, but Sarek (Mark Lenard) and Amanda (Jane Wyatt) were on hand to check up on their son's well being.

Although Steve Meerson and Peter Krikes worked with the whale/time travel story, ultimately it fell to Nicholas Meyer and Harve Bennett to work on the screenplay and bring it to its final fulfillment

At first, Nicholas Meyer was a bit reluctant to be drawn into the project. "I don't know what the first screenplay was, because I never saw it." Meyer explained. "Harve said, 'We don't have a lot of time so here's what we want to do.' And when I heard the story, I said, 'Well, wait a minute, the whole middle of the story is a kind of rip-off of *Time After Time*. I said, 'Do they have to go to San Francisco, I've done that city. Can't they go to Paris?' And they said, 'No, they have to go to San Francisco.' And I said, 'Well, it's even more of a rip-off, then.' So I agreed to do the middle part because, obviously, I've done it before and I'm so familiar with it.

"In fact, there are scenes in *Star Trek IV* that were cut out of *Time After Time*. There used to be a scene in the movie with a punker holding a ghetto blaster. I cut it out of the movie because I didn't shoot it right and Leonard did, so it made it into *Star Trek IV*."

[*ST: TOFCM* #83]

Harve Bennett said that essentially, Nick Meyer took the contemporary scenes and Bennett took the story and framework of getting the crew there and bringing them back home. They did their rewrite in three weeks and then Bennett rewrote Meyer about ten or fifteen per cent, and Meyer rewrote Bennett about ten or fifteen per cent. It was done very quickly, but they had written together before.

Meyer wrote all the scenes on Earth from the time Spock says, 'Judging from the pollution content of the atmosphere, we have reached the late Twentieth Century,' which is his first line in the movie. Harve Bennett wrote the first part of the film up to that line.

(However, Meyer was once overheard describing the writing of *Star Trek IV* at an advance screening. In this offhand version of events, it was divided by humor content, as he told his companions that, while Harve Bennett had written all the serious parts of the movie, Meyer himself had written all of the funny parts! This would seem to be corroborated by Harve Bennett's own appreciation of Meyer's humorous side.)

But as far as historical structure went, having Bennett script the first and last parts of the movie made perfect sense to Nimoy. Again, in *Cinefantastique*, the Vulcan-turned-auteur praised his sometime producer: "There were historical elements that Harve is very good at. He knows how to deal with the Federation council meeting and all those things. What I wanted Nick to do was add his tone, his style and touch to the humor. "

Script problems were not the only delays faced by Bennett, Nimoy and crew; Willaim Shatner decided to play hard-to-get. This situation was one which delayed the shooting of the film. But to an even larger extent, they lost time because of the management change at Paramount, which affected the Shatner situation.

When Shatner finally signed, production on *Star Trek IV* was further delayed by Shatner's contractual obligation to complete the current season of his television police drama, *T.J. Hooker*.

Finally, all these matters were ironed out, and another *Star Trek* shoot was underway.

Crucial to the portrayal of the storyline, were the whales themselves. There is actually only one live whale in the film, and that's the surface shot of it breaching which was done by Mark and Debbie Ferrari. Every other whale shot is a miniature, articulated or mechanical reproduction of a whale's anatomy. There have been many whale pictures but all of them suffered the minute they put the mechanical whales in the film. Bennett felt that the whales looked so real in the film that people didn't realize they were special effects. Maybe that's why the film didn't get an Oscar for the effects.

Nimoy and his team first contacted George Lucas' Industrial Light and Magic in November of 1985. Heading the ILM team were Ken Ralston (visual effects supervisor) and Don Dow (director of effects photography). Design duties were shared by ILM art director Nilo Rodis and visual consultant Ralph McQuarrie, well known for his work on George Lucas' *Star Wars* movies.

In a 1987 *Cinefex* interview, Don Dow recalled his initial approach to the whale problem. "They knew nothing else in the script was going to be a big problem, but they were very anxious as to how we were going to deal with the whales. In fact, they had alternate creatures in mind and were ready to change the script accordingly in case the whales never did work out.

It was just about that time that Humphrey the whale swam into San Francisco Bay— almost as if he had heard we needed whales for our film and had come in to audition. We grabbed our cameras and spent several days chasing Humphrey up in the delta trying to photograph him. All we really intended to do was get reference footage, but Leonard was very excited about the possibility of getting something we could actually use in the film. Unfortunately, that didn't work out because of various difficulties involved. By the time we'd get Humphrey and get our cameras set up, he'd be off to a different spot— and then, of course, we couldn't get in the water with him because he was an endangered species. However, we were able to spend a lot of time observing him, and that helped us considerably."

It was decided that robotics would probably work better than optical processes; in other words, however they were done, the whales had to be "live." To this end, ILM contracted the services of robotics expert Walt Conti, who told *Cinefex* about the creation of the whales of *Trek*.

"It was really quite ambitious to build something like this, totally self-contained and radio controlled. As far as we know, there was no precedent for it. I think [art director] Nilo Rodis figured he had a guy here who didn't know anything about film so maybe he could talk him into it. My biggest worry was whether we'd really be able to control it. I knew we could make [a whale] move and flop around, but could we make it actually go where we wanted it to go? As it turned out, that aspect of it wasn't the most critical. Without much trouble we could hit a foot-square target across the pool in any direction. We had more problems in things like the materials, the skin wrinkling, and such. But it was definitely the most efficient way to handle the whale sequences because we were able to avoid the optical process completely. We were fortunate in that the people behind the film— Harve Bennett, Ralph Winter and Leonard Nimoy— really cared about the quality of the whales. Rather than go the traditional route, they were willing to take the risk and finance the development of a totally new approach to underwater creatures. What we did on this film really opens up a whole new tool chest for directors. In fact, you can't help but wonder how much simpler *Jaws* might have been if it had been done with this kind of approach."

The whales were central to the story, and the script called for very specific moves and angles and lighting conditions that made some of the more traditional options unacceptable. For example, they looked at using real whale footage that had already been shot. It would have been difficult to match that footage to the specific moves called for in the script. Also, there isn't much whale footage in thirty-five millimeter. ILM's first reaction was to shoot a miniature against bluescreen and then composite it into some water plates. But with that process it would've been hard to get any subtlety of movement and the right kind of light interaction. Another alternative was to shoot full-size mechanical whales on tracks. this was done for shots of the whales breaking the surface of the water— but that approach limits the camera to very specific angles and movements and wasn't flexible enough for the underwater sequences.

"In some ways," Conti continued, "my lack of film experience was an advantage on this project, as I had no preconceptions of how it should be done. I knew it would be quite a challenge, though, because it is more difficult to replicate a real mammal than it is to do a fictitious creature. An audience knows, very specifically, how a real mammal moves. I found that the movement could be simplified tremendously by keeping the front half of the whale rigid and having all the motion in the tail and in the pectoral fins. Those were the most important areas and so we concentrated on them. We put together a thirty-inch prototype very quickly to show to Paramount. It had the tail motion and was free-swimming, but it still had an umbilical cord coming out of it for power. We threw that together, filmed it, and showed the footage to Paramount. They loved it. At that point, they were able to relax a little bit and we could proceed with the final design."

Pieter Folkens, of the Oceanic Society did a lot of drawings, and used very specific animal data to proportion the animal. His attention to detail, like in the musculature of the tail, turned out to be very worthwhile to ILM's technicians. Richard Miller did the actual sculpting of the whale model, with Pieter's close supervision to insure accuracy. They decided on a four-foot whale to keep it as small as possible and still have room to fit in the servos and radio gear. They spent a couple of months doing research on the tail thickness, which was an important consideration because if the tail was too thin it would buckle when it bent. If it was too thick, the electrical servos couldn't bend it. It took four to six weeks to work all that out.

The whale miniature ultimately consisted of a three-piece fiberglass exterior, but a problem arose: the delicate electro-mechanical devices in the whale were not well adapted to functioning underwater. Servos and water just don't mix. Conti recounted how the problem was solved:

"We decided it was easier to seal each independent electrical servo rather than try to seal the entire whale. At twelve feet down, one little leak will kill you, so we decided to concentrate on what we wanted to keep dry and just let everything else get flooded. Each fin had to move independently up and down, fore and aft and rotate. It was pretty complex. The tail, however, was quite simple. It was just a universal joint pivot controlled by two electrical servos. It was a real simple hinge that moved up and down and side to side, and all the bending and arc-of-the-tail movement was achieved by the way the skin was shaped. The skin was made from a polyurethane manufactured by Smooth-On. In its normal state it's quite rigid so we had to add a lot of plasticizer to make it flexible enough. The most critical area was the tail. With most material, you shape it like a tail and bend it and you'll get wrinkles. That was especially a problem since we were working in miniature and those kind of wrinkles would ruin our scale. We tried a segmented tail with stretch skins over it— which is typically done with creature tails— but that just wasn't working. Finally, we tried a really thick polyurethane skin cast in a tube and it was perfect. When we pulled it out of the mold it felt just like blubber. So we ended up with a really thick tail, about an inch to an inch-and-a-half thick all the way around. Then we had a thinner front half of the whale— about a quarter-inch [thick] from the mid-point forward— to allow room for the mechanics. We had to cast some inserts into the flippers and the flukes to make them stiff enough to resist the water and yet flexible enough that you could see some kind of deflection. It took some experimenting to find that balance. We ended up putting spring steel into the actual mold and then casting rubber around it. That gave us quite a nice, graceful movement." [*Cinefex*, Feb. 1987]

Microballoons were added to the skin for buoyancy needed to make the whales appear to swim. They also positioned lead weights inside to make it horizontally correct. It had to sit in the water just right in order for ILM to control it. They also built a water pump into it which had an intake right underneath its chin. Since whales have a patch of barnacles on their chins, they were able to disguise the intake using barnacles. The water pump was used to turn the whale. They'd turn the tail to the side and activate the pump and the whale would turn just like a jet boat. The pump also enabled it to dive down or come up in the water.

Conti's team, with cameraman Pete Romano, then filmed the underwater sequences— in the pool at a nearby high school! "Pete would be in the pool all day, shivering, but he'd hang in there until we got the shot. We found that we got the most dramatic shots late in the evening when the sun started to set. There would be shards of light coming down and it was very interesting-looking."

In addition to four "whale wranglers"— two above water and two below— there was need for additional help. They used a couple of divers with video assist cameras to show the technicians the relationship between the cameraman and the whales. But it was difficult to see what they were doing because the pool was murky with diatomaceous earth to simulate ocean water and to help maintain the illusion of scale. Out in the ocean, even in the clearest water, when you see a forty-foot whale, the head may be very clear but the tail will be hard to see. Just because it is so far back, you begin to lose the visibility. So to get that same effect on a four-foot model, they had to have a lot of cloudiness in the water. They also had wind machines going, which hampered the operators' ability to see.

"It was very frustrating. We'd made these whales really maneuverable, and in a clear pool we could do anything with them, but when it came time to shoot, our hands were somewhat tied because we just couldn't see. We learned to be very careful to shoot the whales only at certain angles. Technically, shooting the whales swimming from underneath was a great way to see them because it made them look so much larger. But most people are not accustomed to seeing a whale from that position and so it didn't really work. Audiences are used to seeing these animals photographed from specific angles, and if you deviate too much from that it just doesn't seem real to them. One shot that gave us an especially hard time was when the whales turn to a vertical position to sing their response to the probe. It was very difficult to get them into a vertical position and stop there, all in one cut. So we eventually had to cheat a little bit and use some monofilament to pull their noses down into the correct position."

They were very excited about doing the scene with the whales breaching, or breaking the surface right alongside the crashed bird of prey on which the actors would be standing. Their first approach was to actually breach the miniature out of water with jets of air shooting around it to break up the water molecules. When that didn't work very well they went to a dry approach where the whale was under a thin membrane that had sugar and flour piled on it. The plan was to film that with a miniature tank in front of it and have the whale shooting out behind the tank. They drove the whale upwards with a spring-loaded catapult and it would break through the membrane and throw all the dry stuff into the air. Since whales turn onto their backs when they breach, the rig had a rotation on it as well. The producers decided not to go ahead with it, both for story and budgetary reasons, and they ended up just using some research footage that was shot for them in Hawaii.

Rather than use opticals for scenes in which humans interact with the cetaceans, it was decided to use full, one-to-one scale whale sections, again mechanical in nature. These were done at Paramount by Michael Lantieri and Robert Spurlock; Spurlock described some of these whale sections in a 1987 interview with *Cinefex* magazine. "The tail, or fluke, was the most critical of the sections; it was about twelve feet wide and seventeen to eighteen feet long. Larry DeUnger and I spent two to three weeks going over pictures and books and videos of whales swimming and diving to try and home in on the movement of the fluke as it comes in and out of the water. We did all our tests with quarter scale sticks and paper mounted on layout board to try out the necessary mechanisms and to get the movement that Leonard wanted."

When the whale "waves" to the crew of the Enterprise, a ten-foot long fin was used. Explained Lantieri, "In reality, I think that [waving] movement is to show anger, but Leonard wanted it as a sign of affection and to show the grace with which the whales could move. Then we had another section which was the blow-hole. That was used mainly for scenes at the Cetacean Institute. You'd see flaring nostrils come up, there'd be a blow of air and water and then it would go back underwater. Finally we had a male and female back section, connected side by side, for the farewell shot at the end of the show. Together these sections were integrated into the movie so as to convince the audience that there was an entire whale there. From the beginning, our biggest worry was having enough whale for each particular shot. We had arrived at these four pieces basically by studying the storyboards, and I told Leonard [Nimoy] that he was not going to be able to deviate from those boards too much without its creating a major change in what we were doing. Once he was pinned down to specific shots and angles, we knew that we could make our whale fit the storyboard and do what he wanted it to do."

The whale skins were made off the Paramount lot by Lance Anderson and his shop. After they layered the skins up, Tom Pahk and Robin Reilly went over to help fit them. Any part of the whale that was going to have to bend was reinforced with Danskin leotard material and foam rubber so that the skin wouldn't tear. They then brought the skins back to Paramount and applied them over the fiberglass shells.

Originally, they were going to go up north to a Sea World type place in Vallejo and shoot in a deep tank, but it wasn't ready when they required it. "So we ended up in a four foot deep tank at Paramount. That required some drastic changes for us because the whale itself was six feet high. To get around that problem, we had to dig a hole in the bottom of the tank— twenty by forty feet across and six feet deep— to allow the fluke to dive completely underwater. Even at that, the tail just barely cleared the surface by six inches. Whenever we did a dive, we had to keep it pulled way down so it wouldn't pop back up into the shot," Lantieri explained.

Four hundred feet of steel track was involved in working the whale in in the tank. They couldn't have the track fail in any way, because under four feet of water it would have been very difficult to go back in and fix it. The fluke, the pectoral fin and the blowhole were all on dollies that were pulled through the shot by air motors. To get the shots of the fluke coming up and then diving back down underwater, there were two small humps in the track just before it ran down into the deeper tank. The fluke was powered by two sets of hydraulics. All of the movement for its dive had to be choreographed between Al Rifkin, Larry DeUnger, Bobby Johnston and Spurlock. Bobby Johnston would pull the whale with one air winch. Once it went over the hump, they would add the coordinating fluke movement by operating the joysticks that controlled those hydraulics. Finally, Al Rifkin would have to hit a brake in his air motor to slow it down as it went into the hole since this weighed almost two thousand pounds.

Spurlock (again in *Cinefex*) recalled the final whale section, a full-scale whale head used in the scene where Leonard Nimoy, as Spock, mind-melds with Gracie the pregnant cetacean. "The head had an eye piece built by Stuart Ziff that was cable actuated and moved up and down and back and forth. It also had a small pectoral fin that moved. We took the headpiece to a facility at McDonnell-Douglass where they have a big glassed-in tank that they use to simulate weightlessness for astronauts. The head was hung from very fine wires and then moved across the water with Leonard holding onto it doing his mind-meld. We also floated it a little bit by putting inner tubes inside to give it neutral buoyancy. And since the pectoral fin on one side created a weight, we added an outrigger on the other side to balance it— just a milk crate on the end of a pole with some counter-weights. This was the only whale section that floated at all. Since all the others were mounted on tracks, it wasn't necessary for them to be buoyant."

For the first images of the entity that propels the plot of *Star Trek IV*, Nilo Rodis basically conceptualized of the mysterious space probe that triggers Earth's crisis as somehow resembling a cetacean itself. ILM model shop supervisor Jeff Mann recalled, in a 1986 *Cinefex* interview: "Since Nilo's concept was that the probe looked similar to a whale, we built a prototype that was a cylinder shape with barnacles and whale-like coloring, but still basically just a tube. we capped the ends of a piece of irrigation pipe and installed a mechanism to turn the ball-like antenna that jutted out from the bottom. Our primary probe model was eight feet long, but we also made a small one for the long-distance shots and another big section that was a forced perspective model, about twenty feet long and really wide at one end and tapered back at the other. That was for a Star Wars type shot of the probe coming over the heads of the audience, and it really made it look massive, as if it went on forever."

But ultimately, it was not the mechanical whales or an immense, V'Ger-like space probe that made *Star Trek IV* such a warm and popular experience for filmgoers that year: it was the human interaction within the story that truly gave it its inner drive. There was, in fact, nothing in the way of action in the picture at all; no Klingon fistfights or interstellar phaser battles. As Nimoy pointed out to *Cinefantastique*, "Nobody hits anybody. Nobody shoots anybody. The major violence is when Spock pinches the neck of the punker. In fact, in the original script in the hospital scene when they go in to help Chekov, it was written that Kirk comes in and judo chops the doctor. I said, 'We're not going to hit a doctor!' Instead, I had Kirk put them in a closet and melt the lock."

"[I] firmly believed that we could bring [the *Trek* characters] into the streets of San Francisco and not have anybody notice," claimed Harve Bennett. And he was absolutely on the mark. "And, curiously enough, that's what happened. Even though our people are known as *Star Trek* actors, nobody bothered them. there is nobody in the background pointing at William Shatner. They just thought they were strangely dressed people walking around the streets. As a matter of fact, people tend to look away when they see weirdos these days because they figure, well, that's their business."

This turned out to be a key factor in some of *Star Trek IV's* on-the-street scenes. "My favorite moment in dailies was the way Leonard shot the 'nuclear wessells' scene in San Francisco," recalled Harve Bennett. "Leonard shot that with a hidden camera. In the script it only has Chekov saying 'Pardon me, can you tell me the way to the nuclear wessells?' Well, Leonard directed that scene with one actor, which was the cop, and a lot of passersby. It was like a Candid Camera routine. . . The lady who has the long speech where she says, 'Oh, I think they're in Alameda,' was just walking down the street and walked into camera. We had to pay her and make her join the union. That whole scene was wonderfully spontaneous." [*ST:TOFCM* #55]

This sort of off-the-cuff shooting was close to producer Harve Bennett's heart, for reasons he explained in a 1987 interview. "I've done. . . three movies for virtually the cost of the first *Star Trek* movie. I used three classic television budget saving tricks. The first was what we call 'the elevator show.' That's a show where the whole television episode takes place on one set. You know, the elevator stuck between floors. Sixty-five per cent of *Star Trek II* took place on one set. We got three bridges out of one set. But you can't do that twice in a row. *The Search For Spock* was the classic television 'memory show,' [wherein] one of the principal actors isn't there. He was directing but he wasn't on screen. So we spent the money on the big set for the Genesis Planet. The fourth movie used yet another 'keep the budget down idea' which is called 'local location.' That means you don't build sets, you go out into the streets and shoot outside the studio. If you shoot 'local location,' the advantage is, you don't have to dress it to look like 1940 because our film takes place today. If you make it 1940 then you have to start bringing in old cars and you have to spend a million dollars on wardrobe." [*ST:TOFCM* #55]

Leonard Nimoy was quick to point out the movie's environmental correctness, however. "I'm not a heavy contributor [to Greenpeace] but I get their newsletters and things. The idea of putting the spaceship between the whale and the whaling ship and being hit by the harpoon obviously has Greenpeace origins because that's what Greenpeace used to do to attract attention to the Save The Whales campaign. They went out in rubber rafts in front of Russian ships to prevent them from firing their harpoons. That has always remained in my mind and that's where the idea came from. I didn't set out to do a film about ecology. You can say I'm concerned. But the idea of the whales came because it seemed like a useful and romantic device. if we're helping the whales to get along better in the world, that's great."

[*Cinefantastique*, June 1987]

Bennett didn't think that there was any question that the movie would help a lot of beleaguered organizations like the American Cetacean Society, which is a little-known but most influential save-the-whales group. They were the film's most vocal supporter. Bennett felt that all environmental groups will gain from this film to some extent. They made a conscious effort for the film to say, 'Beware of what you are destroying today because you never know what the implications will be to those yet to come.'

The film's climactic moment occurs when the crew find themselves up on charges for actions dating back to the earlier films. Under the circumstances, the Federation is lenient, and only one person is penalized: James T. Kirk, who is demoted to captain (remember, he's been an admiral in all the movies so far) and forced to take command of a new vessel, which turns out to be a new *Enterprise*, NCC-1701A. Harve Bennett, of course, knew that this had to happen, but claimed that the destruction of the *Enterprise* in *Star Trek III* was not originally planned. It was not in the first draft screenplay of the film. He felt it was an urgent dramatic sacrifice to heighten the need to make a life or death decision. Once he had done that and the movie was completed, he took a quiet oath that he would restore the *Enterprise* in the next film, in just the right way.

As an aficionado of military history, Bennett drew upon his considerable knowledge of similar tactical sacrifices. For example, Oliver Hazard Perry, who said, 'Don't give up the ship. ' In the battle of Lake Erie, Perry takes the flag with him. He scuttles the *Niagara* and in a rowboat with the flag he goes to the next boat and beats them. Then, six months later, he recommissions a new ship and it's called the *Niagara*. So that tradition in the navy came through in *Star Trek IV*.

Nimoy's second outing as the director of a *Star Trek* feature was a job he seemed to relish. "This [was] more my personal film. The last film (*The Search For Spock*) was kind of a movie that we all got together to do; I was the director, and responsible for what got up on the screen, but there was more a sense of people coming together, a sense of collaboration. This is 'A Leonard Nimoy Film' by title, and I took that responsibility very seriously. I feel a greater sense of growth here. I feel that the training wheels have come off.

"We previously had life-and-death situations, and friends of ours dying, and I think we've had enough of that for a while. I also felt that we had done two pictures in a row with a kind of black hat heavy, Ricardo Montalban in *Star Trek II* and Chris Lloyd as Kruge in *Star Trek III*. . .

The TV series didn't depend on black hat heavies each week, and I felt strongly that the films shouldn't be a series of us, good guys, against them, bad guys. I insisted that this picture would not have that kind of tone, and that if there was a problem, it would not be created by a bad person. It would be a problem created by misunderstandings, by ecological problems, by scientific problems, that kind of thing, but nobody with 'no-good' intentions. And in this film, such a problem is discovered, that we have to deal with and solve."

In *Star Trek III*, Nimoy was on his back for two or three small moments, and then on his feet playing one major scene at the movie's end. It was quite the contrary in *Star Trek IV*. There he was on his feet throughout. It was a difficult job and it was for that reason that he turned down *Star Trek VI* when it was offered to him.

"Spock is quite different," Nimoy went on to explain about how his character appears in *Star Trek IV*. "We pick Spock up at the point where we left him in the last movie. He was disoriented, trying to figure out who's who here, until he finally recognizes Jim. So, he's quite a different Spock than we've seen before— he's funny and charming. We see him experience a kind of growing-up process in this picture. He's bemused and wondering. 'What's going on? What am I supposed to do about this?' His memory is back— we find out very quickly that he has been training his memories and feeding himself on large quantities of information, facts, figures, data, history and so on. But, on the other hand, his sensitivities and sensibilities, his awareness of social attitude and conduct and how to function in society, are still a little bit askew. So he's really looking for 'How do I do this?' It was the most fun I've had playing Spock in a long time."

William Shatner, too, had positive reflections concerning this particular outing. "I've been very happy with Kirk's character development. The part of Kirk has always been a challenge. I never get bored with it. Each role, each ti*Star Trek* comes up, it's a challenge to make it good and interesting— alive." Still, there's always the possibility it might go on *too* long, muses Shatner. "The objective thinking is that as each year goes by, as we all age, so does Captain Kirk. And I suppose there is the possibility that I'll wheel myself in, sitting in a wheelchair, and say, 'Press. . . um. . . *that* button there.' The idea is not to fight the aging process. Hopefully, I will keep it at bay for a time to come." [*STIV: The Official Movie Magazine*]

DeForest Kelley was particularly happy with Star Trek IV, and said so looking back on it at the press junket for *Star Trek VI: The Undiscovered Country*.

"I wish that number four had been number one. *That's* the kind of movie! Not necessarily that much comedy, but a human story with very few special effects is what we did an awful lot. The second movie showed that perhaps we might be back on track somewhere because number one wasn't what any of us had in mind for a *Star Trek* movie," Kelley observed. "I think *Star Trek II* was the first spark of, 'This is more like it.' " But Kelley preferred number four because it wasn't as violent as the second and third. "I was very worried about that. I walked out smiling about it, though, and when I got up the next morning, I went and poured a cup of coffee, which I do, and I stand and look out the window for about fifteen or twenty minutes every morning. I got to thinking about the picture again, and a couple scenes in it—Leonard and Bill on the bus and that sort of thing, and I started to laugh to myself. I thought, well, that's a pretty good indication. Maybe it will affect someone else that way. But I still expect it to be picked apart here and there. I think the purists will look at it and say, 'It's too comedic. It's not science fiction. It's not what we like.' "

The only real criticisms one can level against *The Voyage Home* is that for a time travel story, it plays a bit fast and loose with the concept of paradox in that it basically ignores the repercussions the trip would have due to the tampering. For instance, Scotty gives a company the formula for Transparent Aluminum—but what about the person or persons who really invented it? Scotty has changed history. History is potentially changed again, in an even more catastrophic manner, when the Navy gets Chekov's phaser and communicator—containing 23rd century technology. The characters in the film move blithely on their way without calculating any of the consequences of their actions. It's almost as though Bennett and Meyer were saying that since they were writing a comedy, logic could be ignored. But the move did make over a hundred million dollars, so what's a little tampering with the time stream among friends?

With a new ship and the crew still intact, it seemed inevitable that a fifth *Star Trek* film would soon be underway. On April 11, 1986, Walter Koenig let slip to his pal Harlan Ellison on the *Hour 25* radio show that the director of the next installment would be none other than William Shatner. Apparently the studio felt that if one actor could direct, why couldn't another? Or perhaps this was Shatner's idea, rather than the studio's original inclination. Denials flew left and right, but it seemed that Shatner had pretty much made his involvement contingent on having his name stencilled on the back of the director's chair that had been occupied by Wise, Meyer and Nimoy in previous outings. Once the success of *Star Trek IV* was pretty much rock-solid, Shatner blew his cover himself, and confirmed the rumors, and also claimed that the story of *Star Trek V* would be his creation as well. Gene Roddenberry was not too keen on this, but the die was cast, although the ever-diplomatic Harve Bennett did claim that Shatner's assumption of writing credit was a bit premature. But with *Star Trek IV* on screens around the world and raking in the cash faster than ever before, Leonard Nimoy, for one, was ready to relax. The fact that he wasn't going to direct *Star Trek V* was undoubtedly a load off his mind, as he told *Cinefantastique* in 1987. "Sure, I'll act in it, and I'll watch Shatner suffer for a while. Bill is extremely imaginative and energetic and a very bright guy. He'll be a little shaky the first day or two, but he'll quickly find his own style and pace. I have high hopes for it."

But history, with its capricious and unexpected turns, was about to give *Star Trek*, and Paramount, a swift kick in the derriere. *Star Trek* in and of itself was not a magic phrase which spontaneously produced money out of thin air, as the studio was about to learn to its dismay.

In the wake of the huge success of Star Trek V: The Voyage Home, a fifth Star Trek motion picture was a foregone conclusion, and William Shatner exercised what he saw as his right to direct the film. So far as we know, no one objected, at least in the beginning.

FIVE: THE FINAL FRONTIER

"I dream in films. I've always wanted to make a film. I've thought of the episodic television that I've done as short stories in a progression towards a novel. The absolute miracle of being able to direct a large motion picture is now a reality." —William Shatner

As soon as it was clear that *Star Trek; The Voyage Home* was a bonafide hit, discussions began concerning the next sequel. Due to a contractual clause which guaranteed that whatever Paramount offered Leonard Nimoy they also had to offer William Shatner, it was clear that this time Shatner would invoke that agreement so that he could direct *Star Trek V*. Shatner only had directing experience on episodic television up to that time, but since this had been the extent of Nimoy's directing experience as well before *Star Trek III: The Search For Spok*, that wouldn't serve as an obstacle.

It wasn't just a case of Shatner wanting to direct a theatrical film just because Nimoy had, he'd been interested in directing for a long time."I remember having the urge to direct some of the *Star Trek* television episodes," he told Marc Shapiro in *Starlog* #144, "but at the time, I felt directing was beyond my capabilities. After the series, I began directing plays and a number of *T.J.Hooker* episodes, and that gave me the confidence that, some day, I might actually be able to direct a film."

Although *Star Trek IV* had opened in November 1986, it would be at least a year before *Star Trek V* would even begin moving forward, much to Shatner's dismay. At the November 1986 press junket for *Star Trek IV*, prior to his signing the final contract to direct *Star Trek V*, Shatner discussed the fact that it had taken two-and-a-half years to being *Star Trek IV* to the screen and how he planned to get *Star Trek V* made more quickly than that. "Two-and-a-half years is an extraordinarily long time. I hope it won't be that long. I don't see how mine will be that long. It's the rare person who gets to play with $23 million." (The budget was subsequently set at $30 after a production date was set.) "By April, we should have at least the first draft. If we don't, I'll begin to cry. I have a story idea that has met nods of approval from Paramount. So I'm looking for a writer. We're having trouble with negotiations, but by April I will have hired a writer and we will have a script which I hope is along the lines of the story I've been developing."

However, delays arose which pushed back the start date of *Star Trek V* further and further. Leonard Nimoy chose to direct another film, *The Good Mother*, rather than wait for his protracted and complicated contract negotiations for doing *Star Trek V* to be settled with Paramount. Nimoy was fresh from the hit film *Three Men And A Baby* and was eager to work on another non-*Star Trek* project. Then in March 1988, a lengthy strike of the Writer's guild of America hit Hollywood and several months passed before it was settled, although the script for *Star Trek V* had been completed prior to the beginning of the strike.

All through 1987 and into 1988, William Shatner had been developing his story for the movie, which he had first shown to the executives at Paramount in 1986, before *Star Trek IV* was even done filming, as tentative plans for the next sequel were already being discussed at that point.

Shatner's story involved the Enterprise meeting God, even though this was the basis of the original script idea Gene Roddenberry had written in 1975 when Paramount was first interested in doing a *Star Trek* motion picture. In fact, in spite of how many hands came along to shape and reshape the script which became *Star Trek: The Motion Picture*, a lot of similarities to that story remained in the final version. Primarily all religious references were expunged from the old concept. But Shatner's new concept hinged on religious ideology even though it was that very facet which had caused Paramount to openly reject Roddenberry's 1975 screenplay.

Shatner's original story synopsis involved a holy man named Zar who, along with his followers, hijacks the Enterprise in order to go to the center of the universe where God can be found. Along the way Zar wins over the entire Enterprise crew to his cause, including Spock and McCoy, with Kirk being the lone hold out.

The story started out much as the final film did, with Kirk, Spock and McCoy at Yosemite where Kirk has his climbing accident and is saved by Spock. This leads to a discussion of the issues of life and death around a campfire until their shore leave is abruptly cancelled by a message from the Enterprise. A holy man had taken some dignitaries hostage and the Enterprise was being sent to negotiate their release.

The holy man in question is the absolute ruler of a planet whose people follow him fanatically. The followers capture the Enterprise but Kirk hatches a plan to kill the leader, until Spock warns the holy man of the trap. Spock had known the holy man years before and believed it possible that if anyone in the universe could be the new messiah, this might indeed be the man. But Spock is still locked up in the ship's brig with Kirk and McCoy, only now Kirk feels that Spock has betrayed both his captain and the Enterprise.

Zar wins over the rest of the Enterprise crew to his cause, convincing them that they are indeed on their way to solve the oldest riddle of the universe; the riddle of whether God exists. The holy man has a mental power that allows him to uncover a person's innermost secret and free them of its pain. He frees McCoy of the pain of the responsibility for his father's death, and Spock of being rejected at birth by his parents.

The holy man reveals that Kirk has never been truly loved, and is alone except for his passion for the Enterprise. Zar proves his power by healing an old recurring injury in Kirk's knee. Zar then promises to relieve Kirk of the pain of his son's death, once they see God.

When the Enterprise arrives at God's homeworld, Kirk seems to have joined with all the others on their crusade. Kirk, Spock, McCoy and Zar beam down to the planet and find it a flaming world, like something pictured in the drawings from the ancient text of Dante's *Inferno*. God appears to them surrounded by the legendary seraphim and cherubim (the highest order of the angels in Heaven). This seems like the real thing. But while conversing with this supposed deity, Kirk detects flaws in the philosophical veneer, and upon questioning this God on certain points, the being becomes angrier and angrier until the facade falls and it is revealed to be the devil.

Spock and McCoy had been at odds with one another and so when they flee they refuse to help each other, or help Kirk, either. When Spock and McCoy are surrounded by the Furies (which the angels had changed into), Kirk goes to Spock's aid, healing the personal rift between them in the process because he has risked his own life to help him. McCoy is captured and taken to the River Styx. Kirk and Spock rescue McCoy and make it back to the Enterprise.

Shatner's concept went to the very heart of religion and both verified certain basic ideals while challenging others. He described his concept this way: "That man conceives of God in his own image, but those images change from generation to generation, therefore he appears in all these different guises as man-made Gods. But in essence, if the devil exists, God exists by inference. This is the lesson that the *Star Trek* group learns. The lesson being that God is within our hearts, not something we conjure up, invent, and then worship."

Shatner showed this proposal to Paramount Chairman Frank Mancuso, who gave him the okay to develop it further and bring in a writer to flesh the story out into a screenplay. Originally Shatner sought novelist Eric Von Lustbader to write the script, and even flew to New York to meet with him, but Paramount and Lustbader were unable to work out a mutually agreeable contract.

Still in need of a screenwriter, Shatner turned to the equally important problem of signing on a producer for the picture. In spite of the success of *Star Trek IV*, which Harve Bennett had co-written with Nicholas Meyer, Bennett was reluctant to sign on for another *Star Trek* film.

In *Captain's Log: William Shatner's Personal Account of The Making Of Star Trek V : The Final Frontier* by Lisabeth Shatner (and that's the last time I'm going to use that entire unnecessarily long title here), Bennett explained why Shatner had to convince him to sign on to another *Star Trek* film.

"I was not anxious to do *Star Trek V*," he explained. "My reasons were [that] I had been emotionally beat up by Leonard Nimoy. I respect him for what he has done, but in the transition between III and IV, Leonard had come to regard me as in his way, with regard to the auteurship of the film. I was not only the man who said `No,' but the man who was conspiring to...you know. So that on one occasion, it got really mean on the stage — mean from him to me. I was smarting, 'Who needs this shit?', was foremost on my mind. Plus the fact, if you keep doing the same material, whether it's a series or big pictures, you're still doing a series."

Bennett agreed so long as Shatner truly accept him as the producer, as the man who would say no to him and who would voice opinions about the story that had to be listened to. This was of particular importance because the story had been concocted without Harve Bennett's participation and he wasn't very enthusiastic about the search for God concept. As it turned out, Paramount wasn't completely enamored with the story either and questioned whether the plot could be reworked to allow the addition of humor.

This was a particular strong point in the minds of the studio production personnel because *Star Trek IV* had been a breakout film, surpassing the $100 million mark. It was believed that it had done this by appealing to movie-goers outside the normal crowd who patronize a *Star Trek* picture. And the way these people had been attracted was with the humorous nature of the film.

The problem with this reasoning was that *Star Trek IV* had been a humorous adventure, a light-hearted tale with a serious idea at its core. This allowed for humorous scenes and banter throughout much of the picture. But *Star Trek V* had never been conceived of in this regard. By forcing humor into the final product, the story had already begun to be twisted out of shape.

Harve Bennett had recognized from the beginning that even though *Star Trek IV* had done at least 30% more at the boxoffice than the previous two films, that part of the reason for that was for a reason which couldn't be duplicated in *Star Trek V*, the 1980's setting of the adventure.

In the June 1988 issue of the bulletin of the Official Star Trek Fan Club, Bennett explained, "Having expanded the horizons of *Star Trek* awareness in that dramatic of a way we couldn't say, `Well, that was nice for that but now let's go back to what we had before.' You never want to do that. By the same token, one of the reasons for the dramatic success of *Star Trek IV*, above and beyond whatever it was as a film, was that it was contemporary. And, therefore, it crossed a line and brought a lot of people in who had never seen *Star Trek* before. It was essentially a contemporary comedy which had its roots in modern society. So part of *Star Trek IV's* success was the fact that people were saying, `Hey, this is fun! This takes place today and it's kind of funny! These guys have a great perspective on what's going to happen.' And the film became a very special cup of tea. We can't keep doing that, though. *Star Trek V* cannot be another time travel story, as convenient as that would be. So the challenge is: can we keep the broader audience as entertained by what is still *Star Trek* as they were in *Star Trek IV*?" This was exactly what Paramount was worried about.

At the time of the film's production, rumors of Paramount's insistence that humor be added sounded like heavy-handed meddling at its worst. But as it turned out, there was far less humor in the film than expected. The problems which ultimately plagued the film came from a completely different sort of studio interference: money.

In the early development stage of *Star Trek V*, director William Shatner didn't realize that this problem was waiting to ambush him.

In lengthy story sessions with Harve Bennett, the idea finally emerged that "God" would turn out to be an alien falsely claiming to be the deity in order to trick Sybok into coming to the planet to rescue him. This concept came out of a combination of Bennett's believing that the idea just wouldn't work otherwise, and the studio people concerned that doing a story involving basic religious beliefs would offend large numbers of people.

Although Harve Bennett wanted to get Nicholas Meyer to work on the screenplay, Meyer had other commitments at the time and so another screenwriter was sought. David Loughery had just signed with Paramount on the basis of his screenplay for *Flashback*. He'd written other scripts, but *Dreamscape* had been his only foray into science fiction. Bennett and Shatner agreed that Loughery had what they were looking for as a writer and he was quickly assigned to do the first draft script for *Star Trek V*.

Loughery used Shatner's premise as the basis of his expanded outline, with the major change being that God turned out to be an alien who lured them to the planet so that it could escape its long imprisonment there. Paramount approved the outline and Loughery began turning it into a screenplay.

Enter Gene Roddenberry. Although having a reduced role on the *Star Trek* films ever since the critical failure of *Star Trek : The Motion Picture*, Roddenberry still had the title of executive consultant, a role which had no true authority other than his own intimate knowledge of the series based on his nearly twenty-five years of involvement with it. So while Roddenberry couldn't physically interfere with a production, if he objected to something strenuously enough he could threaten to take his name off the film and make sure it was widely known why he had done so. By the time *Star Trek V* reached the stage where Loughery had been given the go-ahead to begin the actual screenplay, Roddenberry's input had not been sought at all, and when he learned that a story had already been approved by the studio, he kicked up a fuss.

Roddenberry's comments on the story outline are interesting, particularly in light of Roddenberry's own swing at "*Star Trek* meets God" twelve years before.

"I thought it was very unwise to do a story which seemed to be talking about God because there are so many versions about what God is or isn't," he said. "And living in a time in which you have Tammy Baker and the young lady who got screwed — not that that's an unusual happening in any religion — I think the public was beginning to see that many religions are nothing but flim flammery, dedicated to getting as many bucks as possible. And I didn't want *Star Trek* to be associated with any one of them.

"The original story I saw was, 'The Enterprise Meets God.' And my point was that it had to be even more obvious [that 'God' is an actual alien]. I didn't object to it being an alien claiming to be God, but there was too much in it that an audience could have thought was really God or really the devil, and I very strongly resist believing in either. I do not perceive this as a universe that's divided between good and evil. I see it as a universe that is divided between many ideas of what is."

Roddenberry also felt that certain incidents violated the integrity of the characters. "I had some objection to McCoy and the others believing it was God. McCoy was saying, 'Hallelujah, I'm with ya, I'm with ya!' and only Kirk and Spock understood the difference. I said, 'Hey, these are people that have been with you for twenty years, through thick and thin, through a variety of things, and I don't really think you serve them well by having them fall on their face and say, 'I believe, I believe,' I suggested he [Sybok] better have some power over them if you were going to have someone like McCoy say 'I believe.' You'd better have some reason to do it."

But the bottom line, aside from Roddenberry's objection to the story tackling religion, was that he was never consulted about the story until he kicked up a fuss. "I created *Star Trek*. I don't take anything away from Leonard or Bill or anyone, but I'm the guy who did it. How dare they start something without listening to my comments, whether they follow them or not? And I've never insisted they follow them. If I had strong objections to the story, I would have stated them."

Following Roddenberry's line of thinking, Bennett and Nimoy came up with an idea of Sybok using a form of mind control, and since he was a Vulcan, it would by a mind meld of a type no longer practiced on Vulcan.

Roddenberry also pointed out that the journey to the center of the universe was impossible as the universe has no center. Plus, Starfleet is still exploring the Milky Way galaxy, of which only eleven percent will have been explored by the twenty-third century.

Meanwhile, William Shatner had to go off to work on a film called *Voice Of The Planet*. In his absence, work on the screenplay continued.

Shatner's initial choice to play Sybok was Sean Connery. But before Paramount could make a deal with him, Connery signed to co-star in *Indiana Jones And The Last Crusade* which would be filming the same time as *Star Trek V*.

The concept of Sha Ka Rhee (the name of the planet where God can be found) was fused with other ideas in Shatner's absence. After screening *Lost Horizon*, Harve Bennett and David Loughery wrote a draft of the story which completely altered the ending so that Sha Ka Rhee was like Shangri-La and this is what they were searching for, a place where no one ever grew old. Sort of like Never Never Land.

Shatner returned from doing *Voice Of The Planet* and was upset after reading this latest version of the story. It took him two days of arguing but he finally convinced Harve and David to return to their original direction for the story.

"*Lost Horizon* is a kind of heaven on earth," Harve explained. "Some of the allusions it was providing us were not the home of creation, the home of the Almighty. They were rather a safe harbor. We were getting our metaphors mixed up. So we pulled back from that." But the concept of Sha Ka Rhee remained, merely its purpose was altered to merge it with the previous ideas.

Nimoy's input on the story had been sought from the beginning. Initially, upon reading Shatner's original outline in which God turns out to be the devil, et al, he remarked, "If you film this you'll be laughed off the screen." Shatner was upset at the complete dismissal of his story but was willing to discuss it, as the changes it went through prove. But one change hit Nimoy the wrong way and he took a long time adjusting to it — the concept that Sybok was Spock's long lost brother. Nimoy wasn't comfortable with bringing a brother in from left field like that. Nothing in the nearly twenty-five years of *Star Trek* had ever established that Spock had a brother. Making him Spock's half brother from Sarek's previous marriage was a compromise he grudgingly accepted.

Since Sybok uses his mindmeld technique to release a person's secret pain, Bennett, Loughery and Shatner had decided that Spock's secret pain was that he had never reconciled the pain of never having been fully accepted by his parents when he was a boy. But Nimoy objected to this idea, stating that Spock had reconciled his half-human, half-Vulcan situation in previous films and so there would be no hidden pain over that for Sybok to release. So Sybok had to have a different way to get Spock to enlist in his cause, particularly since Nimoy felt that Spock's profound loyalty to his Captain would prevent him from betraying Kirk.

Shatner learned of Nimoy's opposition to that sequence of events in the latest draft of the script on the same day that Paramount failed to approve everything Shatner wanted to do in the film, so budget cuts would have to be instituted. The double blow of bad news on the same day caused Shatner to dub it "Black Thursday."

Bennett and Loughery attempted to come up with an alternate reason for Spock going along with Sybok, but Nimoy flatly rejected it, stating that under no circumstances would Spock betray Kirk. Finally the ending was rewritten where Spock refuses to go along with Sybok, as does McCoy, but in the end Kirk, Spock and McCoy accompany Sybok out of curiosity, not devotion. Shatner had wanted Kirk to be the lone holdout left to question the veracity of God, but that angle was written out.

Even DeForest Kelley objected to his scene with Sybok because it involved Dr. McCoy killing his terminally ill father. Kelley thought this went against everything McCoy stood for and it took a long time for this scene to be written to his liking.

James Doohan wasn't enthusiastic about the script either. He told Lisabeth Shatner, "I didn't care for it too much at first, but when we first read through it at Bill's place, I liked it a lot better. I think it's going to turn out very well. To me the best one we've done was *II:The Wrath Of Khan*. Four was fabulous...but I prefer a good drama."

Walter Koenig's comments on the story could be termed possibly damning with faint praise. "I think rather than breaking new ground, it has exploited and maintained ground we know is proven."

At the time, Bennett stated, "I like most of all that it promises to be both entertaining and, in terms of the subtitle, *The Final Frontier*, it promises to get deeper than any man has gone before into the relationship of Kirk, Spock and Bones. It reaches an entirely new level of intimacy forced by the story. What are these men really made of? And what do they really mean to each other? That's the kind of thing that's held *Star Trek* together for so long — those wonderful characters!"

With the script problems worked out to the satisfaction of most everyone involved, it seemed the biggest obstacles in preproduction had been resolved. There had even been a question about whether DeForest Kelley would be able to participate due to an illness he had at the time. Then the budget axe fell.

Shatner had conceived some complicated ideas for the film which, had they been brought off, would have required complicated optical effects to achieve properly. Elements of Shatner's original script ending still remained, including having the angels turn into demons. But due to the complex effects required for this, Shatner decided just to have Kirk, Spock and McCoy chased by six rockmen which rise up from the rocky landscape around them. The rockmen suits would have cost $300,000 to manufacture and never made it into the film.

The budget cuts weren't over yet. When Bran Ferren came back with his bid for doing the effects, it was $5 to $6 million, while Shatner and his team had only budgeted $4 million. Faced with an increase of as much as fifty percent above what they had planned for, further cuts were the only recourse. The entire film was budgeted at $30 million, and to go to Paramount and ask for another $3 million would not have gone over well.

While one would think that a $30 million film could afford a $6 million effects budget, you must realize that Shatner and Nimoy were receiving about $4 million each. As much as Shatner agonized over the scenes he had to cut from the effects budget, at no time did he apparently ever consider kicking back some of his salary to make up for the shortfall, even though he was the director and this film would reflect on his abilities more than any other single motion picture he'd ever appeared in before.

The decision to go with Bran Ferren for the special visual effects had been made during the months the production sat idle during the 1988 Writer's strike. Executive producer Ralph Winter had originally wanted to go with Industrial Light & Magic, whose vast facilities had provided such fine work on previous *Star Trek* films, but by the time ILM was contacted, they were already booked solid to such films as *Ghostbusters II*, which also had a June 1989 release date to meet. So it was finally decided, after considering various companies, that Associates and Ferren, located in Long Island, New York, would produce the crucial opticals. These would include the shuttlecraft crash-landing in the hanger bay, as well as the Great Barrier surrounding the planet Sha Ka Rhee and the God creature itself. Complicating this was that Ferren's company had three months to produce the necessary opticals, which is half the time a major film usually allows for such complicated effects.

Regarding his experience on *Star Trek V*, Ferren stated in the May 1990 issue of *Cinefex*, "There were many effects I would have liked to have done more imaginatively, but we were in a panic mode just trying to get everything done. We were previewing the film three weeks after the director had his cut. We were cutting negative before we even previewed. If we had not done that, we would not have made the deadline. That kind of schedule is a nightmare. If there had been six months of post, Paramount could have previewed it, decided there were fundamental issues that needed to be corrected and perhaps made a better movie. Given our time squeeze and budget restrictions, the final effect of the project could have been much worse. Overall I was happy with what we created. What we produced for *Star Trek V* was admirable — perhaps even miraculous under the circumstances. I just wish we could have had a year."

Shatner had gone into this project with great enthusiasm. There were ideas he wanted to put on the screen; things he wanted to accomplish. "It was my story and so I was already thinking about what I wanted to do visually with it. I know what I like to see in a picture. I wanted this to be a film in motion, an action-packed film in which the camera is never still and where exposition is covered by something in motion. There are also things

I like about directors like David Lean, Martin Scorsese and Walter Kill that I've taken, reinterpreted with all the influences in my life and put into this film." But not all of Shatner's visions were to make it to the screen. Early in preproduction, when the script was being analyzed for budgetary purposes, what the director had previously regarded as key shots were among the first to go.

Scenes cut included earth as seen from space and other powerful establishing shots. When Kirk was climbing El Capitan in Yosemite, the camera was envisioned to pull back and back until Kirk became a small dot on the mountainside. That was cut as being a shot which alone would have cost $350,000. When the effects were cut to the bone, a day was cut from location shooting, putting further pressure and time constraints on the director. Although Kirk, Spock and McCoy are seen in the film on shore leave in Yosemite with no one else around, Chekov and Sulu originally had scenes showing them on shore leave at Mt. Rushmore (but also filmed at Yosemite) including one where they glance up at Mt. Rushmore and we see that it has an additional face carved into the rock alongside the old presidents — that of a black woman who had been president. The scene was to show Chekov and Sulu wandering around lost, whereupon the camera pulled back to show them at the foot of Mt. Rushmore. But preview audiences didn't get the joke of the extra head and weren't laughing, perhaps because they thought they were supposed to recognize who the fifth head was and were confused when they couldn't.

Interestingly, the cut scenes, which must have seemed like luxuries or extras at the time, turn out in retrospect to be the kind of extra personal touches which would have combined to add something to the film. With them cut, the film's special effects come across as being wild and inconsistent — from the excellent model work and photography of the Klingon bird of prey to the cheap looking effects used to show the alien who pretends to be God.

In describing the cuts at the time, Shatner was more prescient than he realized when he explained how their loss would affect the film. "And, something that really hurt, we had to cut down on the number of extras for the Paradise City battle scenes. I had dreamed for so long of shots where hordes of soldiers pour into the city, that it was very hard for me to accept this particular cut. I felt like this grand, epic movie I had envisioned had suddenly been reduced to an ordinary film. When I walked out of the meeting, it took me a while to realize that the movie in my head would not be the movie on the screen. It was my first big lesson as a director." As the director, Shatner planned to bring his own vision to the picture in a number of ways, including in the style of the film, which would involve having a lot of action and movement.

"I have in mind to use action cameras, for lack of a better term, using hand-held cameras, for close impact cuts in the kind of style that I've learned from the streets of Los Angeles shooting action shows," he revealed in the May 1987 issue of *Starlog*. Since *T.J.Hooker* episodes often consisted of a great deal of running and jumping, he stated, "If we could combine running and jumping with some of the other basic tenets of *Star Trek*, it could be equally entertaining." Interestingly, during production of *Star Trek V,* Leonard Nimoy was asked what made this film different with Shatner as a director, and he replied, "It has a lot more running and jumping."

Shatner had also envisioned a darker, grittier look for *Star Trek V* and the art director who helped him achieve this was Nilo Rodis. Nilo had worked on *Return Of The Jedi, Star Trek III* and *Star Trek IV.*

Nilo and Shatner envisioned what would have been two of the most impressive scenes in the film — had they not been cut for budgetary reasons. Said the director, "Nilo and I envisioned the shuttle's entry into the God planet as a magical, fantastical journey. I had seen some paintings by an artist named Bierstadt, who came out of the Hudson River School of painting. These paintings were of mysterious mountains, shrouded in dark, misty clouds — eerie yet inspiring. I knew I wanted that look for the movie, so Nilo and I spent some time discussing what it should be and we came up with some great ideas. We called this `The Bierstadt Shot.' Another great shot we envisioned took place in the very first scene of the film, as Sybok is laughing and the camera moves into the sun. It moves further and further away until it's in the galaxy, then turns around and does a move into the earth, the image getting magnified larger and larger by powers of ten, until it reaches America, then California, then finally into a hand on a granite rock. And we called that shot `The Powers of Ten' shot."

During preproduction, the film was plagued with other problems beyond the control of anyone involved. For instance, one morning it was discovered that someone broke into the Paramount lot and took $60,000 worth of costumes from a trailer. The fact that the trailer was unmarked made it evident that the thief was working on inside information to know what was inside of it. The year before, another theft of *Star Trek* costumes was solved when the thieves were caught red-handed attempting a second theft. Those thieves had turned out to be wealthy youths from Beverly Hills who also happened to be *Star Trek* fans and had learned where some original costumes were stored.

The special effects make-up man on *Star TrekV* was Kenny Myers. Aside from the alien masks and make-ups, Myers also constructed the suit for the rockman.

The production designer for *Star Trek V* was Herman Zimmerman, who had also served in that capacity for *Star Trek: The Next Generation.* Shatner had seen the sets for the TV series and been impressed.

The interesting thing about the connection to *The Next Generation* is that Shatner had been one of those who was suspicious of the need to create a new and different *Star Trek* television series. In the May 1987 issue of *Starlog* (prior to the premiere of the new television series), Shatner states, "I think it is a mistake. To call a series *Star Trek* that doesn't have the cast and the ship in it is an error. The error seems to me to be overexposure of the *Star Trek* name and the possibility of not having the *Star Trek* quality we've become accustomed to. It remains to be seen."

Like Nimoy, he didn't believe that the combination of factors which made the original *Star Trek* popular could be repeated. After all, no other science fiction television series had come along after *Star Trek* which had demonstrated anywhere near its staying power and wide acceptance. Only *Star Wars* had managed to create a science fiction universe which was as arguably as popular as *Star Trek*. Today the staying power of this George Lucas creation remains in question, although some very carefully crafted attempts are being made to revive it to some level where it can sustain itself. The comparison is a valid one because *Star Wars* also generated a massive merchandizing boom, although it began to fade some time after the 1983 release of *Return Of The Jedi* when it was evident that no new films were forthcoming to feed the need of the fans. Only a few novels and some lush art books were issued based on the *Star Wars* films (better art books than *Star Trek* ever generated, for some reason), but today none of those remain in print while the market for *Star Trek* books has, if anything, increased.

On the *Next Generation* front, in 1988, Shatner was still suspicious of the show, which was then in its first season preparing to go into the second. A much discussed incident at the time occurred when young Wil Wheaton, a longtime *Star Trek* fan, visited the Paramount Studios set for *Star Trek V* during filming. He introduced himself to Shatner (who at that time had claimed never to have watched the show), and the actor/director was surprised to learn that Wheaton was actually a cast member on the show. When Wil told him that he had a position on the bridge now, Shatner began ridiculing the boy, stating that he'd never put a child on the bridge of the Enterprise. Wil was reportedly quite upset over the incident and told Gene Roddenberry about it. Roddenberry told Bennett about it, who convinced Shatner to apologize to Wheaton. This was supposedly not the only time Shatner ruffled feathers during this time, and whenever something like this was brought to Roddenberry's attention he'd tell Harve Bennett, stating, "Shatner is your problem now, not mine."

Initially Shatner had not approached his daughter, Lisabeth, to write the making of book on *Star Trek V*. In fact he had drafted an agreement with a writer named Linda Simeone, whom he had met while filming *T.J. Hooker* on the Burbank Studios lot. She had in turn, based on his letter of intent, secured a publishing contract from Pocket Books. Linda was on hand during the earliest days of preproduction, including the period when Nimoy dismissed Shatner's original story outline for *Star Trek V*.

Shatner had told Linda Simeone that he wanted her to do a "making of" book which really told what it was like to make a film, warts and all. He told her everything that was happening, both good and bad, and even upset Harve Bennett by giving her copies of private correspondence between Shatner and Bennett involving an incident between Shatner and James Doohan in which Doohan reluctantly agreed to apologize to Shatner (even though Doohan felt Shatner was in the wrong) because he believed that *Star Trek V* would be the final film and he saw no point in creating lingering bad feelings. When she began writing up her notes into a first draft which Shatner read, he found that the truth came across pretty brutally on the printed page. Shatner decided that he didn't like what Linda had written and wanted to replace her. He also wanted Linda to turn over all her notes on the book, which Linda refused to do unless paid for her efforts.

In spite of the fact that Lisabeth Shatner's book is by no means a tell all history of all the behind-the-scenes shenanigans, it is more honest than similar books as it includes candid observations of some of the problems, as well as Harve Bennett's explanation of why he was reluctant to produce *Star Trek V*

Describing what production was like, Harve Bennett stated in the April 1989 issue of *Starlog*, "During the first few weeks of filming, Bill Shatner shot himself in the foot time after time. It's a different game being in front of the camera than behind it, and directing multiple episodes of *T.J. Hooker* didn't immediately prepare him for the wide screen and its demands. It took Bill time to graduate from an actor and television mentality to a director and motion picture mentality. A year of verbalizing things to him did not have the impact of the first few days of *Star Trek V* film cut together. We were in the viewing room and Bill would turn to me and others and say, `That doesn't work.' Those brave ones among us told him it wouldn't work and then his response had been, `Why are you so bound by rules?' We reminded him in that viewing room that we had been doing this for 30 years and that we knew what worked.

"Bill turned out to be a quick learner," Bennett observed, "and after that episode, he was able to assess what was real and necessary to make *Star Trek V*, rather than what was appetizing. At that point he began to become a director."

As production on the film progressed, so did the typical (and atypical) problems involved with location shooting. Shatner was very concerned about making the film look realistic, something which would only be accomplished by shooting on location. Trying to duplicate exteriors with indoor sets always looks obvious on film.

The major location shooting would be in the Mojave Desert where Paradise City was being built. The town used as home base during location was Ridgecrest. From there it was easy access to the three sites they'd be filming on. Those three sites were Owens Dry Lake bed, where Paradise City was built. Trona Peaks, where the scenes on the God planet could be filmed. And Cuddy Back served as the location for Sybok's opening shot in the desert. On Owens Dry Lake bed, construction commenced on Paradise City, which took five weeks and $500,000 to construct, with the workmen sometimes having to tolerate 100 degree heat.

To achieve the look Shatner wanted for the film, he hired Andy Lazlo as cinematographer. Lazlo had worked on such films as *Streets Of Fire* (directed by Walter Hill, whose work Shatner admired), *Remo Williams*, *First Blood*, *Innerspace* and *Poltergeist Two*. The cinematography is one of the most vital aspects of a motion picture, because if a scene isn't shot well, is poorly lit or done hurriedly, the film looks not only bad, but cheap. One of the reasons the *Star Trek* television series from the sixties holds up so well is the cinematography.

Shatner did a great deal of physical preparation for his directing duties. He ran, lifted freeweights, and worked with a physical therapist. But physical therapy couldn't prepare him for the day to day problems ahead, as his experiences actually directing the film were difficult almost from the start.

On the first day, he filmed the commercial seen playing on the viewscreen in the bar. And on the second day he directed Harve Bennett in full Starfleet uniform as the Commander ordering Captain Kirk to undertake the mission to rescue the hostages. While Bennett was fine delivering his lines, the technical display next to him kept acting up. Then he had to film the scenes with George Murdock, and with Larry Luckinbill as Sybok. Then it was on to location in Yosemite and the mountain climbing and camping scenes.

It was while preparing to leave for location shooting the following day that Shatner truly came face to face with the full responsibilities of the motion picture. "That night was very tense for me," Shatner explained in the July 1989 *Starlog*. "I've always had a great capacity for denial, and even though I had been preparing for this film for a year-and-a-half, I had blocked out the pressures that directing it was going to entail. But that night, I suddenly realized that we were going on location the next day and that there would be hundreds of people asking me hundreds of questions. The prospect of having to come up with hundreds of answers made me awfully nervous."

Cast and crew left for location shooting on October 11, 1988, nearly two years after *Star Trek IV* had opened in theaters. Aside from the delay in 1988 caused by the Writers Guild Strike (which was late in preproduction), the script was still able to be made ready in the weeks before filming began in the fall.

What had actually kept the film from starting sooner was Leonard Nimoy's decision to direct *The Good Mother* while contract negotiations with Paramount dragged on for *Star Trek V*. Shatner had been disappointed by this, knowing that it would push production of his film back many months. Nimoy suggested that Shatner just make the film without him, whereupon his co-star exploded, "You know I can't do *Star Trek* without Spock!" So William Shatner reluctantly accepted the cards fate had dealt him and spent the time working on various preproduction activities of the film while waiting for Nimoy to finish directing*The Good Mother*. *The Good Mother* opened in December 1988, during production of *Star Trek V*, and unfortunately met with mixed reviews and indifferent box office response, unlike Nimoy's previous non-*Star Trek* outing, *Three Men And A Baby*. Nimoy's subsequent film, *Funny About Love*, also had poor box office response.

The day everyone left town for Yosemite, other problems faced them. The film studios had been struck by the Teamsters Union, which meant that the trucks carrying wardrobes and equipment had to be driven by largely inexperienced non-union drivers. A camera truck had been blown up on the Paramount lot, but no injuries resulted. Under cover of darkness, the convoy of trucks left the Paramount lot, escorted onto the freeway by police as vehicles carrying men whose faces were masked followed the studio trucks and threatened them verbally and with shaking fists.

Location shooting was plagued with problems, including footage which didn't come out as intended. For his climbing scene, Shatner had himself rigged up with a safety harness so a camera angle could be gotten showing that he really was three thousand feet up on a mountain, but after all that effort, the footage was unusable due to shadows on the ground from clouds and a lack of anything between Shatner and the ground to give the sense of perspective. Other problems included trucks breaking down as well as a truck arriving at Ridgecrest in the late afternoon and finding no one around to tell him where he had to be or when to be there.

Miscommunication like this was a constant problem largely caused by the inexperienced drivers who didn't understand the purpose of everything they were carrying in the trucks even after being told what it was. While Hollywood certainly has experienced non-union drivers, they had been snapped up by the other studios as soon as the Teamsters strike was called.

Even off the set Shatner found himself faced with surprising problems. At dinner one night with his daughter, Harve Bennett, Ralph Winter and Nilo Rodis, a woman shrieked and leaped into Shatner's lap, overturning his chair and spilling them both on the floor. The young woman ran out of the restaurant while Shatner was still composing himself. After the hardships of location, they were actually able to find the bizarre incident humorous.

Upon returning to Los Angeles, principal photography continued at Paramount Studios, and so did the problems. The first in-studio shots involved the shuttlecraft crash into the landing bay. But this particular sound stage had a storage vault underneath it, so the floor was too thin to support forklifts or any such machinery which would ordinarily have been used to position the full scale shuttle mockup. Because of this, the shuttle had to be positioned by hand and the logistics of this cost them seven hours of shooting time.

Shooting inside the shuttlecraft was cramped and presented additional problems until Shatner decided to hired a Steadicam cameraman which enabled the shooting to go faster. Other problems resulted from using rear projection of the space scenes on a screen outside the shuttle window. The delays mounted and the schedule fell three days behind.

This was further aggravated when two days of shooting seemed to be lost due to a scratch on the film, but optical effects expert Brad Ferren saved the day by showing how the film image could be blown up and cropped. Had this problem not been solved in this way, Shatner would have had to repeat two days of shooting. Even before this incident, Paramount had been putting pressure on the director to catch up.

When he had lost time filming because of a projection machine involved in the rear projection of a scene outside the shuttle, one of the studio heads approached Shatner with a warning; that if they lost any more time, they'd have to cut pages from the script to make up the schedule. "My initial reaction was anger at being put in that kind of position, and from that point on, I found I was being tugged mentally in two different directions. The people around me, who had been connected with *Star Trek* a long time, were telling me not to worry about it, that they always tell you those things and that if you make a good picture, they'll forget about the time. On the other hand, I was being told by the studio that they were going to cut my script!

"I started to sweat," Shatner recalled unhappily. "When an actor was five minutes late getting to the set from the makeup trailer, my stomach would start turning. Finally I decided that this may be my lone opportunity to make a big budget movie and I may ultimately fail miserably. I resolved in my own mind that I was going to enjoy every second of the experience, including the tensions, not to get overwhelmed by the filmmaking process and to just do the best possible job I could."

Events moved more smoothly on the Klingon bridge set, which Shatner had envisioned being cramped like the interior of a submarine. When he saw the long corridor which had been attached to the rear of the bridge, he decided to film the scenes there with the connecting door open in order to give the scenes more depth and give the impression that this small room really was a part of something larger.

Todd Bryant and Spice Williams, the two main Klingons in these scenes, took their roles so seriously that they were even coached in official Klingon dialogue so that they could deliver their lines in both English and Klingon. They were tutored in this by Mark Okrand, whos efforts at developing a Klingon language had been published as the official *Klingon Dictionary.*

The scene in the barroom, when we meet the hostages, was originally longer than the final cut. The dialogue omitted was largely humorous character dialogue involving the old Klingon, Korrd, making rude remarks to Caithlin, the Romulan ambassador, and her final and equally colorful replies. For instance.

CAITHLIN

I'm here to open discussions for a solution to these problems.Korrd comes to life. He roars with laughter and spits back a disgusting mouthful of Klingon. Talbot winces.

CAITHLIN

(losing patience)

What did he say? I want his exact words.

TALBOT

He said the only thing he'd like you to open is your blouse. He's heard Romulan women are different.Caithlin's embarrassment turns to anger.

CAITHLIN

You tell Consul Korrd — never mind. I'll tell him myself in the only Klingon I know.Caithlin lets loose with a Klingon epithet. No translation necessary.Sputtering with rage, Korrd hurls his flagon aside and clambers to his feet.

KORRD

(in perfect English)

Screw you, too!

CAITHLIN

He does speak English!

TALBOT

(surprised)

Sly old bugger!

One of the many aliens in the bar sequence is the cat lady, whose body makeup was devised by Kenny Myers. Aside from the body stripes, the Cat Lady (played by Linda Fetters) also had three breasts. In order to accomplish this, Kenny Myers had to take a mold of Linda's, ahem, chest area so that the third breast would fit comfortably between the other two and match them.

Following these scenes with the Cat Lady, including Kirk's fight with her, they went on to do some additional shots of Spock carrying Kirk by the foot to match with the El Capitan mountain sequence.

The last scene filmed was actually one of the first scenes in the movie (as well as the last), the campfire scene. Shatner felt this was important because it stressed the family-like relationship of Kirk, Spock and McCoy.

When these scenes were finished, they broke out the champagne to celebrate and the following week held an official wrap party at a restaurant in the San Fernando Valley. There's no indication that anyone jumped into William Shatner's lap this time. But just because principal photography was completed by no means meant the film was over. Extensive post-production followed in which Shatner chose which takes of the many scenes he wanted cut together and then worked with the film editor Peter Berger on the pacing of those sequences.

Shatner's first cut of the film was two hours long, which was before the addition of opticals and end credits. This was considered too long for what Paramount wanted and so Harve Bennett stepped in to examine the film and make more changes.

"As I was watching the film, I realized Harve had done a lot of things to the movie, some of which helped it and some of which I simply did not agree with," Shatner explained. "A good example of how he helped it was the army sequence, in which I had included many stunts and long fighting sequences in my version. Harve had cut it down so that we only see the army overwhelming the town, which got to the point faster and was more ideologically consistent with Sybok's character. But I felt that some of the more important moments had been changed. For example, the opening sequence where Sybok's hooded figure comes riding into frame had been shortened dramatically. Also, I noticed that the nine A.M. shot of the mountain at Trona was gone. I felt that these were two of the more important moments in the film, since they went a long way towards giving the movie an epic quality which it otherwise lacked. I realized at this point that Harve and I would have to work out a compromise position with which we could both live."

When the film was edited to everyone's satisfaction, and nearly all of the complicated optical effects were in place, a test screening was held for a preview audience. Unfortunately the reaction wasn't as enthusiastic as they'd hoped for. Only a fraction of the audience rated the film "excellent," and so a discussion was held with some of the audience members to explore their problems with the film.

Aside from problems with pacing, some questioned Spock's wavering loyalty throughout the film. They also questioned why the Klingon would rescue Kirk. To resolve this dilemma, an additional scene was quickly written by Harve Bennett and shot by William Shatner on board the bird of prey showing that Korrd had exerted his authority over Klaa, and this is when Klaa apologizes to Kirk. This then cut to Spock in the gunner's chair, which in the context with the new scene went further to underscore Spock's risk to save Kirk. There had been rumors when *Star Trek V* was released that the new footage shot involved the scene on the Enterprise with the old ship's wheel where Kirk, Spock and McCoy discuss the meaning of what they've gone through, but that was not the case. Additional editing on the film solved the pacing problems which the test audience had complained about.

A second audience test screening was held after the new scene was cut in and the additional editing was made on the motion picture. This one was far more successful than the first preview screening. The audience loved it.

But not all the audiences loved it when it was released. The film received mixed reviews, both from fans and critics. People seemed to either love it or loathe it. The special effects, particularly those involving the alien on the God planet came in for particular criticism. Some fans found the campfire scene corny beyond redemption. The film grossed only $50 million in the United States, which was disastrous as *Star Trek* fans have to recoup more of their costs in America than most other films because the series isn't as popular overseas as *Star Wars*, *The Terminator* and other film series are. After the $100 million grosses of *Star Trek IV* in 1986, *Star Trek V* was considered quite a comedown. Some attributed this to a possible overdose of *Star Trek* due to the weekly *Next Generation* television series, but that sounded more like second guessing, and the existence of the series certainly didn't hurt the box office performance of *Star Trek VI* in 1991. Part of the problem was that June 1989 was a big month for film openings. Even *Ghostbusters II*, a much anticipated sequel, underperformed next to the runaway success of what turned out to be that year's most eagerly awaited film, *Batman*, which went on to do five times the business of *Star Trek V*.

"It didn't make as much money as the others. It fell about eighteen percent short," Shatner explained, looking back on his experience two years later. "But apparently that was the first summer that these blockbuster movies were released every two weeks and *Batman* came shortly thereafter. So the tendency is to blame the release pattern rather than anything else. As for notices and things, in fact it did get good notices." But as to how Shatner ultimately viewed it he stated, "I thought that it was flawed and that I didn't managed my resources as well as I could have. And I didn't get the help in managing my resources that I could have. I thought it was an interesting story and an interesting attempt at a story. I thought that it was a meaningful play. It carried a sense of importance about it. Technically it went well, I thought. We hired a lot of different people; we didn't go after the Lucasfilm people. We experimented and I had to learn a great deal, not only about film but about the politics of film on that picture. I don't think I'll make those same errors again." But the experience did not discourage Shatner from wanting to direct a motion picture again. "On the contrary. It's made me froth with ambition."

In November 1991, at the press junket for *Star Trek* VI, Nimoy was asked how he judged William Shatner's work on *Star Trek V*, and he candidly replied, "He worked very, very hard. He directed it as well and as capably as I think any of our other films, but he was not riding on a good script, and if you're not riding on a good script, you as a director are the one people will point fingers at, and he was responsible; he helped develop the script. It was his story. But he was not riding on a good script. I had that experience. I finished a film for Paramount last year that didn't work at all. I wasn't successful with the script." At the end, Nimoy is referring to the 1990 movie he directed called *Funny About Love*. "I complained," Nimoy continued, explaining about what happened on *Star Trek V*. " I said I think you've got some problems here, and the message I got back was, `We know what we've got, and we know what we want to do.' And having sent in my notes about my concerns, once they got them, it's not my place to say you must do the following."

Due to the unenthusiastic reception of *Star Trek V* in the summer of 1989, a year would go by before plans for the sixth film were finalized and approved in order to get the picture out in the twenty-fifth anniversary year of *Star Trek*.

Leonard Nimoy

Leonard Nimoy at his Hollywood star ceremony
PHOTO © JAMES VAN HISE

And behold, there came a silver anniversary, and they looked down from atop their Paramount view and said, "Let the cash cow deliver!"

SIX: UNDISCOVERED COUNTRY

George Takei has suggested that *Star Trek VI* happened because the timing was more than merely opportune, it was right on the money.

"Some of the marketing people discovered that 1991 happens to be the silver anniversary of *Star Trek*. What a great opportunity to market t-shirts, medallions, stamps, underpants—all sorts of things can be sold—except you need a vehicle. You need another movie. And so that's what saved us despite the disappointment of number five."

In January 1991, *Star Trek VI: The Undiscovered Country* was described by the returning Nicholas Meyer, who was slated both to write and direct the feature, as "a small story about Spock in love."

Guess again; *Star Trek VI* has nothing of the sort in it. True, it does in fact feature a brand new female Vulcan character portrayed by Kim Cattrall, but it now seems that the much bandied-about Spock-in-love rhetoric was somewhat of a smoke screen, apparently designed to conceal some big surprises in this latest entry in the ongoing tale of the Enterprise and her crew. But this is not bad news; *The Undiscovered Country* is a breath of fresh air after the clumsy confusion of *Star Trek V: The Final Frontier*.

A gripping new adventure, in the wake of the all-but-disastrous *Star Trek V: The Final Frontier*, the Nicholas Meyer-directed *Star Trek VI: The Undiscovered Country* delivers all the goods we've come to expect (or at least hope for) from the series: action, character, suspense and a moral tone closer than ever to that of the late Gene Roddenberry's original *Star Trek* concept.

Where *Star Trek V* fumbled, *Star Trek VI*, released close behind Gene Roddenberry's passing, manages to go the whole hundred yards and more; it is fortunate that Roddenberry was able to see the finished product before his death. Word is that he was quite pleased with the final results. If *Star Trek VI* is the last mission of Kirk and his crew, it is

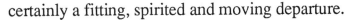
certainly a fitting, spirited and moving departure.

The movie begins, literally, with a bang, as Captain Sulu and the crew of the *U.S.S. Excelsior* (just back from a mission cataloguing gaseous anomalies in a remote sector of space) witness the destruction of the Klingon moon Praxis. (The fact that Sulu commands his own ship is one fact that slipped through Paramount's security precautions when James Doohan spilled the beans at a convention; studio executives in attendance were rumored to have stopped breathing temporarily.) Several months later, it is revealed that this disaster on Praxis is wreaking an ecological catastrophe that threatens the Klingon empire with destruction. Spock is on hand to break the news to Kirk and the others: the Klingon Chancellor Gorkon, who has made the first move towards a much-needed peace with the Federation, is going to come to Earth, and Kirk and the Enterprise are going to bring him there.

Not surprisingly, it was Leonard Nimoy who came up with this scenario once he was approached by Frank Mancuso of Paramount to do another *Star Trek* film. The political situation in the film mirrors, on a scaled down, simplified level, the drastic changes taking place in the world as the Twentieth Century nears its end.

Specifically, Nimoy was inspired by the on-going demise of the status quo in the Soviet Union (which in fact ceased to exist several weeks after the release of this movie). Of course, such radical change brings fear: many, the world over, wonder what these alterations in the fabric of our civilization will bring in the new century (or sooner), even as they welcome the end of systems they long believed to be evil or inefficient. And as in the Gene Hackman thriller, *The Package*, elements on both sides realize that their power is dependent on the maintenance of the status quo, and they struggle blindly— even in collusion with their enemy equivalents— to stem the tide of history.

"When Paramount asked me to come up with a story idea," recalled Leonard Nimoy, "I felt that it would be interesting to go with an idea that had to do with current events in the world. I also wanted to come up with something that would give the Enterprise and its crew some sense of having finished the essential mission. There was a lot of closure— that was the intention, to do a closure with the Klingons. That was exactly what I suggested."

William Shatner liked the idea as well. "It's a classic *Star Trek* idea in that the important issue of the day is incorporated into the story of *Star Trek*. By doing so we're able to comment on it as though it has nothing to do with today."

"It was clear to me that what Ronald Reagan had referred to as the 'evil empire' was coming apart," Nimoy explained, "and was going to have to reach out and create some kind of detente. The Berlin Wall had come down. I had been to Russia and seen the whole *glasnost/perestroika* kind of impact, and I thought, there's going to have to be a lot of dialogue—there's going to have to be a new kind of rethinking of these relationships.

A whole new military vision. A new vision about hardware. So I thought what an ideal way for us to have our closure, too, because the Klingons, for us, were the Communist Bloc—the evil empire. So it just made sense to do that story. We may have an appeal for a foreign audience that we never had before because of the issues."

With this idea in his mind, Nimoy approached Nicholas Meyer. The directorial responsibility could have fallen on Nimoy's shoulders for a third time, had he so chosen (funny— no one asked William Shatner to helm a second *Star Trek* epic!), but Nimoy felt, after his efforts on *The Voyage Home*, that directing *and* donning the necessary Vulcan makeup appliances would be much too stressful a task, especially in addition to his new executive production duties.

"Directing *Star Trek IV* was very tough for me because Spock is a two hour makeup job, and if you add that to the double job of acting and directing in the film anyway, I just didn't want to do it any more."

Nimoy stepped into his newfound production role in the wake of Harve Bennett's departure. Although Bennett produced *Star Trek V*, his interest in the series had long been waning, due in no small part to acrimonious exchanges between himself and Nimoy as far back as during the production of *Star Trek IV* when they clashed because Bennett, as producer, disagreed with decisions made by Nimoy, the director.

Another primary reason for Bennett's departure was the fall-through of his planned *Starfleet Academy* picture, a prequel which would have examined the youthful James T. Kirk at Starfleet Academy and the entry of Mr. Spock into human society. Needless to say, this would have involved new, younger performers in the roles created by Shatner and Nimoy, although they may have appeared in a framing sequence, had the film ever been made.

Part of the problem here may have been negative fan reaction. The title of the project brought up images of the dreadful *Police Academy* comedies, even though the script by David Loughery (with Bennett) was quite serious, focussing on the development of James T. Kirk from a callow young daredevil to a serious, risk-taking potential leader of men. Paramount's Ned Tanen, had given Bennett the green light on the project, but the rest of the studio executives shied away from the notion.

Part of the story would have involved a struggle against slavery somewhere in the galaxy, Bennett's tribute to Gene Roddenberry's early courage in attacking racial prejudice. But apparently Roddenberry, much less the studio, did not recognize the tribute as a tribute; Spock's own trials at the Academy would have echoed the anti-racism theme, but it was not to be. Also lost is the tale of Kirk's first love and the tragic events which forever mold his character. Gone also is any opportunity to see what sort of a job Harve Bennett would have done directing the project.

Bennett has not been idle. He's been working on a movie script, and may return to television work for ABC, the network for which he created such hits as The *Six Million Dollar Man* and *The Bionic Woman.*

Nicholas Meyer threw himself into his scripting duties for *Star Trek VI* with great enthusiasm. This time around, he co-wrote his script with a new collaborator, Denny Martin Flynn, who had long served as Nicholas Meyer's assistant. Appropriately enough, the two scripters kept in touch by means of a computer hookup.

Once the script for *The Undiscovered Country* was completed, there was still the matter of who was to direct the film. Meyer hadn't even considered directing while he was involved in the process of writing, as that occupied all of his attention. Apparently, directing a second *Star Trek* movie had never even entered his mind until after his wife had read the screenplay; her opinion, expressed directly to him, was that he *had* to direct it, and that no one else could. Meyer couldn't easily argue with that sort of input!

As might easily be expected, Meyer jumped when Paramount Pictures offered him the directorial helm for what would be the second *Star Trek* film to bear his imprimatur. Meyer was probably also influenced by a string of unsuccessful films that he'd directed in the wake of *Star Trek II—Volunteers, The Deceivers* and *Company Business,* a cold war thriller released just two months before Star Trek VI opened.

This news was good news as far as the cast was concerned, especially in the case of DeForest Kelley: "[Nicholas Meyer] knows everybody's lines in the script, and if somebody forgets a line, he doesn't have to refer to the script at all, no matter what the line is. Even the speeches. . . whole speeches. If the actor isn't present to do your close-up off camera, [he] can stand back there and recite the lines to you."

Of course, this directorial assignment gave Meyer an opportunity to gaze back on his first outing, *The Wrath of Khan,* still a favorite in the series with countless fans and devotees. "I haven't seen it in a long time," he admitted in an officially released magazine profiling the film. "'I've always been proud to hear that the fans consider it one of the best in the film series. At the same time, I'm totally daunted by my present circumstances in which I'm going to be compared to something that has assumed this kind of place in the sort of mythology of *Star Trek.* There's no question that we'll fall short at least in the first blush because it will be new and it won't be the same."

As usual, Meyer approached the *Star Trek* series, and the *Enterprise* itself, from the viewpoint of the nautical tradition. "My view of the Starship *Enterprise* has always been a cross between a destroyer and a submarine. If I were designing spaceships for *Star Trek* , I would probably have designed a much more claustrophobic world because it's more dramatic. Gene Hackman once told me his theory that the best acting takes place in very enclosed places. I think there is a certain interesting theory to that remark. I don't know that it's always true but it's sometimes true. . . I shrunk the corridors [of the Enterprise] on that theory."

Meyer's only point of reserve was, ironically, one that centered on special effects. 'They're really hard because I have such little interest in them and I have to force myself to really concentrate. . . it's always fun, though, to see the special effects shots starting to come in." [*ST:TOFCM* #83]

Once Nicholas Meyer was officially at the helm, another *Star Trek* voyage was, at long last, underway. Constant rewrites kept on polishing and refining the story as shooting progressed, with continual input from Leonard Nimoy. The subtitle for the film, proposed by Meyer himself, was in fact his originally selected subtitle for *Star Trek II*, which was almost known as *The Undiscovered Country* instead of *The Wrath of Khan*.

Meyer explained in a fan club interview just what it was that he had in mind: "*The Undiscovered Country*, which is a flowing, romantic and mysterious title. . . becomes even more mysterious if you recognize the allusion from whence it comes. And it just so happens that, in [a] slightly different context, the name is as applicable to *Star Trek VI* as it was for *Star Trek II*. *The Undiscovered Country* comes from one of Shakespeare's most famous soliloquies." [*ST:TOFCM* #83]

If not in fact the Immortal Bard's *most* famous soliloquy, most recently tackled on film by the Road Warrior himself, Mel Gibson:

To be, or not to be: that is the question: Whether 'tis nobler in the mind to suffer the slings and arrows of outrageous fortune, or to take arms against a sea of troubles, and by opposing, end them?

*To die: to sleep; no more; and, by a sleep to say we end the heartache and the thousand natural shocks that flesh is heir to, 'tis a consummation devoutly to be wished. To die, to sleep; to sleep, perchance to dream: aye, there's the rub. For in that sleep of death what dreams may come, when we have shuffled off this mortal coil, must give us pause. There's the respect that makes calamity of so long life; for who would bear the whips and scorns of time, the oppressor's wrong, the proud man's contumely, the pangs of disprized love, the law's delay. The insolence of office, and the spurns that patient merit of the unworthy takes, when he himself might his quietus make with a bare bodkin? Who would fardels bear, to grunt and sweat under a weary life, but that dread of something after death, the **undiscovered country** from whose bourn no traveller returns, puzzles the will, and makes us rather to bear those ills we have, than fly to others that we know not of? Thus conscience does make cowards of us all; and thus the native hue of resolution is sicklied o'er with the pale cast of thought, and enterprises of great pith and moment, with this regard their currents turn awry, and lose the name of action.*

—Wm. Shakespeare, *Hamlet,*

Act III, Scene I

The quote itself is first made reference to in the pivotal dinner scene.

Walter Koenig recently revealed a behind-the-scenes glimpse at the shooting of this scene— too bad there wasn't a blooper reel. "Because almost everybody had dialogue in the scene, they had to shoot it an inordinate number of times.," Koenig disclosed. "And, during the course of those thirty-five or forty times, everyone got a little punchy. Leonard, Bill and DeForest had the term 'Starfleet' in their dialogue, and at least once during the thirty-five takes, they all said 'Star Trek' instead, which of course is absurd. 'Star Trek' never crosses the lips of a crew member, because that's the name of the whole thing. It got hysterical. Each of them would laugh at the other when he made a mistake, and they would make a mistake in turn.

I was very fortunate. . . I didn't have to say the word 'Starfleet.' " [*STVI:OMM*])

The basic thrust of the scene is this: A reluctant Captain Kirk, bound by his diplomatic mission, is dismayed when Chancellor Gorkon, his daughter and officers actually *accept* his polite but unenthusiastic invitation to dine aboard the *Enterprise*. At this point, an Enterprise officer makes a menu selection that will prove ominously significant in the light of approaching developments: why not loosen things up with some highly potent Romulan ale? And it is with Romulan ale (yes, its that puzzling pale blue liquid people were always drinking out of square glasses on the television series) that Chancellor Gorkon makes a toast to "the undiscovered country": the future. The dinner is a stressful but intriguing social failure, as two disparate and hostile cultures strive to communicate on a personal level for the first time, and Kirk and his officers are exhausted by the time the Klingon contingent returns to its own vessel.

A careful examination of Hamlet's soliloquy, wherein the melancholy Dane decides to fight his overwhelming troubles rather than commit suicide, reveals that the undiscovered country in question is actually a description of that unknown territory which one might enter after death. . . not the future for the living.

It seems that the Klingons themselves appreciate Shakespeare, and that they have their own unique personal interpretation of his work. (Actually, one would probably find that the honor-ridden but violent Klingons would prefer the plays of Christopher Marlowe, or, better yet, John Webster, whose labyrinthine and bloody drama *The Duchess of Malfi* would have been right up their alley.) General Chang, one of the dinner party, even goes so far as to quip that Shakespeare is best appreciated in his original tongue, which Chang insists is Klingon; he 'proves' this point by reciting another part of the soliloquy—"To be or not to be"— in his guttural native tongue. And the sanguine Klingons, unlike the denizens of Earth, might in fact not make such nice and precise distinctions between death and the future as we might: the two, to them, are probably merely two different aspects of one and the same thing.

On the other hand, Chancellor Gorkon doesn't manage to see much of the future, which certainly calls into question the validity of his reading of the phrase in question.

Shakespeare, it seems, was much in the minds of the creative team behind *Star Trek VI*, particularly where the Klingons are concerned.

"[The Klingons] all look very regal and very Shakespearean," confirmed DeForest Kelley, musing on the British actors cast in the two key Klingon roles. "They're marvellous characters. David Warner and Christopher Plummer— excellent actors— have a great deal to do in this film. [Christopher Plummer] was a delight. He has a wonderful sense of humor. He is, as we all know, a true professional, and I found it a joy to work with him." [*Starlog*, December 1991]

In casting David Warner in the pivotal role of Chancellor Gorkon, the farsighted (albeit short-lived) visionary Klingon leader who realizes that his race's survival depends on shedding some part of their cultural burden of hostility and aggressiveness, it seems highly unlikely that Nicholas Meyer had any misgivings whatsoever. After all, Warner had played Jack the Ripper (against Malcolm MacDowell's H.G. Wells) in Meyer's first great filmic success, *Time After Time*. He was a natural choice for the part.

Originally a stage actor, David Warner made the transition to film early in his career when, at the age of twenty-two, he played a villainous cad in Tony Richardson's filmic adaptation of Henry Fielding's classic novel *Tom Jones*. This provided him with quite a bit of typecasting— not to mention steady work, a fact which amuses him somewhat. "Perhaps because I'm thin and cadaverous looking— pop me in black and make me the villain!"

However, he didn't always play heavies, and has had parts in such notable films as Alain Resnais' *Providence*, with John Gielgud. Other memorable David Warner performances can be found in such movies as *Morgan*, Sam Peckinpah's *Straw Dogs* (with Dustin Hoffman), *The Omen* (where he made a rather spectacular exit), *TRON*, and *The Company of Wolves*. His typecasting in villainous roles perhaps reached its culmination when he essayed the personification of Supreme Evil in Terry Gilliam's *Time Bandits*. He also had a small role in *Star Trek V* (but not as Gorkon.)

In addition to showing the kindler, gentler side of the Klingon people in *The Undiscovered Country*, David Warner also adds (along with a few other Klingon cast members) a bit to the many shades which make up the palette that is *Star Trek*— when we learn, rather dramatically, just what color Klingon blood is. (Fresh, it's sort of a day-glo purple, fading to a somewhat less vibrant magenta hue after exposure to the atmosphere.

Yes, a specter of treachery arises and slays the noble Gorbachev— er, Gorkon. A mystery arises, too, as he is killed by two heavily suited Starfleet personnel who beam over to the Klingon vessel after the Klingons' artificial gravitational system is temporarily disabled. Who on the *Enterprise* could be involved in such dire plottings? Hard to say (until later, anyway). But it doesn't take much heavy thinking to realize that General Chang, conveniently "missing" during Gorkon's assassination, is linked to the Klingon side of this perfidious scheme. It's painfully obvious. One might question Gorkon's interpretation of certain Shakespearean passages, but at least he was consistent, concise and stuck to the point whenever he quoted from Shakespeare.

Chang, on the other hand, goes hog-wild (or the Klingon equivalent) with the quotation bug. He flings out, almost as non sequiturs, line after line from the works of the Elizabethan dramatist. He *has* to be the bad guy, if only so Kirk and crew can shut him up somewhere closer to the end of the movie.

But all this villainous hamming is impeccably done, since General Chang, the other key Shakespearean Klingon in the picture, is portrayed by the estimable Christopher Plummer. He is a Canadian actor with a long and distinguished career which began in Britain's National Theatre when it was under the direction of Laurence Olivier. Plummer has had roles in such films as Nicholas Ray's *Wind Across The Everglades* (Plummer's first screen role), *The Sound of Music*, *The Return of the Pink Panther*, *The Royal Hunt of the Sun* (with the late Robert Shaw), *The Night of The Generals*, John Huston's *The Man Who Would Be King* (as Rudyard Kipling), and *Murder By Decree* (as Sherlock Holmes, with James Mason as his Watson).

Meyer was inspired to cast Plummer, not by seeing one of his film or stage performances, but by hearing him on a record.

"[There] was an album that came out of the music of the William Walton [score for] *Henry V*, with Plummer doing various lines of Shakespeare from the film. It is a great, great, recording. I listened to this and was reminded of how brilliant this guy is that I wrote the role for him. And he had worked with Bill Shatner at Stratford, Ontario— Bill had been his understudy. And as Chris said, 'I knew he was going to be a star because he went on one night instead of me in *Henry V*, and he did everything different.' He was really thrilled and tickled to do it. I think he had a great time doing the film.

Meyer does, however, recall that there was one thing that Christopher Plummer most emphatically wished to avoid: "He said, among other things, 'I don't want a great big forehead!' "

Anyway, General Chang finally manages to reappear, but only after the Enterprise appears to have fired photon torpedoes at the Klingon ship during the course of the assassination. When Kirk and McCoy beam over to try to straighten matters out, they find Gorkon dying; McCoy's futile attempts to save the Chancellor's life are turned against him and Kirk when General Chang orders their arrest for the assassination of Gorkon. Fortunately, Spock had the presence of mind to slap a viridium patch on the back of Kirk's uniform.

This doesn't stop the entire Enterprise crew (and the rest of the Federation, to boot) from being obliged to watch the Klingon kangaroo court that is called into session in order to try Kirk and McCoy for their alleged crime.

The prosecuting attorney in this show trial is none other than General Chang again, who goes a bit easier on the Shakespearean allusions but hogs the spotlight nonetheless. Apparently, despite the obvious bias here, Klingon jurisprudence seems to have some structural similarities to our own, as Kirk and "Bones" McCoy are provided with a legal defense. Perhaps the Klingons have a corps of public defenders. At any rate, the poor schlep who gets stuck with this thankless task is one Colonel Worf, who looks remarkably like his namesake on *Star Trek: The Next Generation*. This is not merely because the character is, according to Paramount publicity, the grandfather (or great-grandfather) of the resident Klingon of the Enterprise-D; this Worf, like the other, is portrayed by actor Michael Dorn. Dorn didn't have to try to hard to land this role; Nicholas Meyer simply dropped by the *Next Generation* set one day and basically handed Dorn this role in *The Undiscovered Country*.

"All roles should come so easily," observed Dorn. "The role was developed out of an idea that Leonard Nimoy and Nick Meyer came up with for *Star Trek VI*. It involved a lot of Klingons. I don't know if it was just an idea or if they were trying to tie the two series together. They decided that Worf would be the logical choice. On *Next Generation*—we had already written things about Worf's parents being on Khitomer, where the peace conference takes place. So, it was a logical, easy choice." [*STVI:OMM*]

Worf's grandfather is the only real reference in the film to *The Next Generation*. There is one other glancing reference in the form of the planet Khitomer, later to be the site of the events that would lead the *Next Generation's* Worf to be raised by humans and to eventually join the Federation.

But despite grandfather Worf's best efforts, the two Federation officers are condemned as assassins and soon are destined to be imprisoned on the harsh penal colony world of Rura Penthe. Once they're there, all they need to do is to get past the penal colony's shield so that the Enterprise can detect the viridium patch. . . which proves to be a bit on the difficult side.

It was difficult for Shatner, the actor, as well. "Some of the physical things were tough. Shooting at night is always tough and shooting at night for a long period of time is tough, and shooting at home, rather than on location, is even tougher, in that the house continues on the day schedule and rhythm and you start work at six in the evening.

"The snow sequences were particularly rough," Shatner explained, "not because it was cold, but because it was warm. We did it on the set and the plastic that we used was particularly odious and since I had to roll around in it a lot, we were coughing it up for weeks ."

Meanwhile, back in the movie, Spock has surmised that the torpedoes supposedly fired by the Enterprise earlier, actually came from a cloaked Klingon ship which was sufficiently advanced technologically to be able to fire while cloaked. His protegé Valeris, an eager junior officer if ever there was one, leads the search for the assassins, which hinges on a pair of gravity boots with telltale spots of magenta blood on them.

Through Valeris, Nimoy felt that he could further show the changes that Spock has undergone over the course of the six films because even though they are both Vulcans, there are very fundamental differences between these two characters.

"In six I think he really is breaking in new ground," Nimoy asserted, "saying to Valeris—'Logic is the beginning of wisdom, not the end.' The unspoken sentence is: It's not even as important as I used to think it was. So I think he's come quite a distance. There was an attempt to change the character a lot in the first *Star Trek* movie. In that movie, I was trying to find a way of establishing the idea that Spock was the living alter ego of that V'ger-thing out there. It was on a search for an identity and Spock could understand that because Spock recognized that he was consciously going through that same process and empathized with this thing. So that was the beginning of that process. In *Star Trek II*, we had a pretty straight-ahead Spock until he died. In *Star Trek III* we had a very different drama to play—Spock was hardly there until the very end and then there was nothing really operating except, 'Your name is Jim.' That's all this great mind could accomplish. *Star Trek IV* was kind of a redevelopment of the whole internal life—the ideas, education, philosophy and everything.

"At the end of *Star Trek IV* I felt that Spock had arrived at a different condition than he'd ever been in before. He was on his game with his father and able to stand toe-to-toe and say, 'I know who I am and I'm not threatened by this relationship any more. I've grown up and if you can't accept that I'm still okay about it. It's no longer my problem.' In the beginning of the movie his mother says to him, 'You will have feelings because I'm your mother and I'm human.' In the beginning Spock doesn't understand what she's talking about. At the end of the movie, his father says to Spock, 'Do you have any message for your mother?' and he says, 'Yes, tell her I feel fine.' So he's using his father as a message carrier to say 'I have feelings' and the father doesn't understand what he's talking about, but Spock is okay.

Star Trek V was kind of an anomaly because the script called for Spock to be forced into a kind of throwback posture, dealing again with the pain of his miscegenation (the Vulcan father, the Earth mother). But coming out of it again okay because he's said, in effect, to his brother, 'I'm not the kid you left behind twenty-five years ago. I've changed. I'm different.' It's playing these changes that have kept me interested."

By now, of course, it's no secret that the lovely Vulcan Valeris, portrayed by Kim Cattrall, is in fact not on the side of the good guys but has been one of the conspirators all along. Her presence was quite skilfully manipulated to seem to be the long-promised romance in Spock's early life. "Leaks" indicating that Spock's wedding, referred to in passing in the "Sarek" episode of *Star Trek: The Next Generation*, would be the culminating scene of this movie, proved also to be false. Allegedly, Jean-Luc Picard's presence at that ceremony was to be one of the links to *The Next Generation* appearing in *Star Trek VI*; but this was not to be.

It is almost impossible not to wonder at how much of this was, almost certainly, conscious manipulation. Once one actually sees the movie, there is, apparently, no indication of Valeris' complicity in the murder of Gorkon, until her involvement is revealed, at which time certain previous scenes and actions take on additional meaning.

But to look back at those scenes is to realize the depth of Nicholas Meyer's writing craft, as the viewer's initial reaction to each scene still seems valid. Even on a second viewing, Valeris' sudden intrusion on a conversation between two crewmen expressing racist views about the Klingons seems to be an instance of a superior officer somewhat coldly diverting a subordinate's attention back to his duty instead of focussing on improper thoughts; certainly Valeris, a true Vulcan despite her choice to conspire with Chang and his ilk, is above racism. That she would be actually sending them to kill Gorkon seems almost, if not absolutely, unthinkable.

Seemingly innocent, also, is Valeris' casual suggestion to Kirk that he serve some contraband Romulan ale at dinner. Who could imagine at the time that such a simple menu suggestion could have such far-reaching consequences when Kirk and McCoy come to trial and are accused of having been drunk? Meyer skilfully diverts us, but without cheating; we also forget that Valeris came into Kirk's quarters just after he wearily expressed his anger, and that she could have recorded his words, until she is revealed as a traitor.

And on one level, it is our expectation of a Spock-Valeris relationship that blinds us to the possibility that she's not on the side of the angels. But even beyond that is this basic, overwhelming fact: she is a *Vulcan*. Vulcans are, and always have been, the ultimate good guys. And this is the crux of Nicholas Meyer's point: things are not always what we expect. Klingons can be noble, self-sacrificing and farseeing, even though there will always be Klingons like Chang who live down to our every villainous expectation. But the moral quality of sentient beings cannot be determined by race; this has long been a cornerstone of the *Star Trek* philosophy, and we are faced with this from another angle when Valeris' activities are revealed.

Just because Vulcans are generally positive characters and always (and sometimes exasperatingly) logical, why should we expect that every Vulcan's logic will lead him or her to the same benevolent conclusions as all other Vulcans? Face it; it just ain't logical! After all, *Star Trek V* had introduced a Vulcan who had deliberately forsaken the modern philosophy of his people.

But still. . . in the previews for *The Undiscovered Country*, the expectation of a Vulcan romance was obviously used to manipulate the audience, by using part of the two-Vulcan mind-meld scenes in such a manner as to suggest that it's some sort of intimate gesture. (Which, even in its real context, it is.) And Nimoy's comments on his approach to Spock almost make no sense once Spock is deprived of his big, long-promised meaningful relationship with a significant other:

"There's a different Spock here. This is a Spock who, having pulled himself back from the dead and back to life in *Star Treks II* though *V*, is now going off into a new kind of personal experience. It's something new for this character. . . Spock has always been a rough character to get a complete handle on. In a way, he's like mercury. Every time you think you know the character, up pops a side of him that you never knew existed. This is a very deep creation, and I think part of Spock will always remain a mystery."

[*STVI:OMM*]

A mystery, yes, but he hardly seems *that* different. True, he is surprised to learn of Valeris' defection, and pained by the process by which he probes her mind, but this is not a radically different Spock here, not by a long shot.

Valeris, on the other hand, *is* a radically different Vulcan from any we've ever seen before. It is a pity, however, that Valeris' reasoning behind her defection is not revealed in any depth; what course of logic led her to make the fateful choice that she did? A Vulcan is not likely to undertake such a serious and risk-laden course of action without first thinking it through in detail.

Of course, a Vulcan who was half Romulan might not be so meticulous. In early versions of the script for *Star Trek VI*, the female Vulcan was not Valeris, but was in fact Saavik, whose choice would have had something to do with the death of David Marcus, who was murdered by Klingons on the Genesis planet. But Nicholas Meyer wanted Kirstie Alley for the role, not Robin Curtis; when Alley proved uninterested or unavailable, he altered the character, and ultimately cast Kim Cattrall in the part.

Interestingly enough, Kim Cattrall tried out for the role of Saavik in *Star Trek II*, but lost out to Kirstie Alley. And she may even be referring to the fact that the role in *Star Trek VI* was originally meant to be Saavik in a recent interview: "[Valeris] was initially named something else. I thought that they should go for a name that was steeped in mythology, so I suggested Eris, which is also the name of the [Greek] goddess of strife. [Nicholas Meyer] came up with Valeris because we wanted it to sound more Vulcan-like."

Cattrall also touched upon Valeris' hidden depths. "She's much more dimensional than just the beautiful woman with the backswept hair who wears the funny ears and a sexy top. I think she's much more defined and has much more succinct desires and wants. She's ambitious. There's really nothing ambivalent about Lieutenant Valeris. . . she has a role in her life, and she wants to do well and fit in— sometimes a little too much."

"It's a very mythical Zen thing, being a Vulcan. It's quite a trip; you really get into it. It's very sexy, too. Vulcans are so smart. There's no excess; it's just enough. Sometimes, as a human, you get so discombobulated with emotions. this was easier because it was so clean to play; it was very clear."

As for the Vulcan mind-meld between Spock and Valeris— now revealed as Spock's drastic means of obtaining some life-saving information from his recalcitrant protegé-gone-bad, Kim Cattrall points out that this was an original procedure, so to speak. "It has never been seen before between two Vulcans, and we didn't know what it was going to be like. It was actually an idea of mine as to what it could be like and feel like." And right or wrong, Kim Cattrall has created a truly memorable Vulcan character, one who challenges our basic expectations about Vulcans, and reminds us that no one can be regarded as morally superior just on the basis of their race

Kim Cattrall was born in Liverpool, England but moved to Vancouver, British Columbia, Canada as a kid; from Shatner to Doohan, and from Christopher Plummer to Cattrall, there has always been a place for Canadians in the *Star Trek* universe.

Kim Cattrall started her professional acting career in the United States with roles in such television programs as *Columbo, Quincy,* and *Starsky and Hutch,* after years on stage in Canada. She began work in such films *Porky's* and *Police Academy.* She's also appeared in John Carpenter's *Big Trouble In Little China, Mannequin, Masquerade, Midnight Crossing* and *The Bonfire of the Vanities.*

As *Star Trek VI* ends, order is restored as is the good names of Kirk and McCoy, and the bad guys are rounded up , including the Romulan ambassador; some *Star Trek* aliens will have to wait another generation or so before they (or some of them) can start to seem redeemable as well. And, in an odd bit of bureaucratic timing, it seems that Kirk and his crew are all demobilized at once. . . but they take another spin around the galaxy for old time's sake, with Kirk uttering the words Nicholas Meyer had originally intended to have his say at the end of *Star Trek II: The Wrath of Khan:* "Second star to the right, and straight on 'til morning."

And so it ends, if we are to believe that there won't eventually be another adventure for this best-beloved crew of of the Enterprise. There is a certain poignancy to their pre-credits sign-off, and there was, by all reports, good cheer on the set from the word go to the day shooting wrapped. But there was, according to DeForest Kelley, no sense of a mournful farewell: "Someone on *Good Morning America* asked me if there was a sad quality or something when we wrapped, and I said no, it really wasn't. It was a feeling of just walking away from something that you had done as if you would be back. There was no formality— nothing really final— everybody saying, 'This is it; it was really good to have worked with you.' We didn't have that at all."

Nichelle Nichols explained that they didn't really have a traditional last day of shooting. "The last day of shooting we went right into a *Good Morning America* interview on stage. We had all of the champagne and food and so forth, and then we had a big photographic opportunity, and then the next day we had to come back and get into makeup and do another photo session. So it kept going. I guess the most poignant feeling was, for me, the first day, because going into six with the understanding that it was definitely the last *Star Trek* film. So we were adjusted to that, and then some of the shinier brass from New York started flying in and we started hearing about the dailies being so good and the next thing you knew we started getting rewrites. The ending was rewritten to make it more open. Even giving one of the characters his own ship opens doors. George is in seventh heaven! He's got his own ship—*Don't stop me now!*

"I would love to really see them move on and expand and then they could really get into some character development with Uhura being back on Earth the head of all communications," Nichelle observed, "and, as I always say, and then she could tell everybody where to go! Rather than confining to the Enterprise and its voyage, spread it out."

The actual filming of *The Undiscovered Country* provided a few adventures of its own, not to mention some surprises for audiences. One of the surprises is the cameo by Christian Slater, a popular young actor who has starred in such films as *Robin Hood, Heathers, Young Guns II* and *Kuffs*. "He did everything he could to lobby to get to be on the set," George Takei revealed. "That was his big dream. My childhood dream was to swashbuckle in Sherwood Forest—he did that—but his dream was to wear the Starfleet uniform. He was literally a twenty-one year old kid in his fantasy land."

DeForest Kelley had his own adventures on the film, such as during the resuscitation scene which was plagued by unusual problems as well as a potentially serious accident.

"When I read the scene I knew it was going to be a difficult scene to do and it's the first time I ever asked a director to go to a set with me before we got on it and just look at the situation and know exactly what's going to go on before we get into it. It's also interesting to me and appealing to me because all of the modern instruments didn't mean a damned thing and he goes back to the old fashioned way of trying to bring this man around well enough to say something, and the complete frustration and the horrible feeling that he has when he loses. So it was a very difficult scene to do.

"We almost had a tragic accident on that," Kelley revealed. "There was a huge lamp up above, a long flat light. When you're shooting you spend all day on that for two days and when I was trying to bring David [Warner] around and pulling these punches, this light exploded and plate glass came down and just missed my neck—hit my shoulder—and dropped so close to David's head that it was just a miracle that neither one of us got cut on the neck or his head split open. The light got so hot under the huge bulb in there that the plate glass exploded. They right away got it fixed and they took awhile to come back. I was back giving him this hit again, and in the course of it my fist hit him and it busted my knuckles and the blood started to come out of my knuckles and I saw this blood as my hand came down and I forgot about pulling the punch and I hit David so hard on the chest that his eyes just popped open. I really brought him around! They kept shooting it, but it was tragically funny.

Despite key cast members and Paramount insisting that the series had come to an end, fans refused to accept the decree. History and random comments lent them solace.

SEVEN: FUTURE IN QUESTION

A cloud hangs over the future of STAR TREK movies. Although official word is that there will be no more films of the original characters, many hints to the contrary have been floated.

Producer/actor Nimoy had high praise for his long time companions, but sounded as if he was tolling the death knell for the movie series. "Everybody went to work with a real sense of gusto. Everybody understood the story. They each have their moments in the script and knew what had to be done. Everybody was very clear and excited about what would be required of them.

"You've got to understand that making *Star Trek* movies has always been like getting together for a family reunion. When we got together this time, we all knew this was going to be the last family reunion. There was a lot of emotion attached to this one, because we knew we were never going to do this again."

William Shatner echoed this sense of finality: "It was a very pleasant experience filled with nostalgia even in the act of making it, realizing that I would probably not work with these people again, especially Leonard Nimoy and DeForest Kelley, who are old friends," he said in an interview at the press junket for *The Undiscovered Country*.

Shatner had finally come down on the side of this being the last movie with the original cast, in spite of comments to the contrary published months earlier in *TV Guide*.

"This is definitely the last one. No question about it. The studio says it's the last one. It's written as the last one. The cast has accepted it as the last one, and it is definitely the last one." When asked if he personally has finally had enough of this after twenty-five years, Shatner stated, "It isn't like it's been in my life on a continuous basis. It comes and it goes and you ride each wave as it comes in. No, I'm still able to find the set. Some of the other actors are too old to find the set," he said, facetiously. "But I suppose that in their wisdom, if the studio thinks that it's time to call a halt to it and give it a finale, I'm agreeable to it and this is the last movie."

Interestingly enough, it seems to be the primary stars who are ready to let the series pass on to the *Next Generation* or beyond; perhaps their success and fame are guarantees of income the supporting actors do not entirely share. Leonard Nimoy, William Shatner and George Takei each received a star on Hollywood Boulevard, and in December '91 and January '92 DeForest Kelley and Nichelle Nichols joined their comrades on the Walk of Fame. But for now they seem to have more of an interest in future *Star Trek* projects than Nimoy or Shatner do. In fact, at the press junket for the film in November 1991, just two weeks before its release, the actors were anything but in agreement on the future of the film series.

George Takei was particularly eloquent when he recited the rocky road the *Star Trek* movies have actually followed.

"The very first film was titled *Star Trek—The Motion Picture,* with the suggestion that that's *it.* That's the movie. That was released, did mega- business, and so they started talking about the only sequel, because sequels generally do about eighty percent of the business of the preceding one, and they didn't think *Star Trek* would do that, but nevertheless, it stands to make some money. So number two was supposed to be the last one—so final that we killed off Spock. And you can't imagine *Star Trek* continuing without Spock. That was released—it did mega—business! So then they started talking about a trilogy; that was kind of trendy at that time. But that means three—it wouldn't be a trilogy if they did more. Number three was supposed to be the very last one—so final that you saw the Enterprise go down in flames. That was the real end, because that was the real star. You can't have *Star Trek* without the Enterprise. That made two tons of money. So then you started hearing about the last *Star Trek,* the final one, number four. And now we've done six and that's what they're telling you again—the last one. Stick around till the end of January when the box office is in—then you'll start hearing about the ultimate, very final *Star Trek VII!*

"Let me also cite something else," George continued. "The denouement scene at the end, on the bridge, where the Captain of a torn and tattered Enterprise thanks the captain of that majestic craft, the starship Excelsior. And then he roars off into the galaxy. And McCoy says, 'My God, that's a big ship!' And then Scotty chimes in with, 'Aye, but not so big as our captain, I think!' Now I think that's a pretty wide open end." And deliberately so, as a closing monologue in which Captain Kirk would talk about turning the Enterprise over to a "new Generation" was replaced at the last minute, thereby deliberately leaving the movie open-ended.

Ever hopeful, Walter Koenig has suggested in the official movie magazine issued on *Star Trek VI* that there was more finality in the original shooting script but that lines were changed to accommodate the possibility of a sequel. "There were some changes in dialogue," he has said, "and the way the movie ends now, there's a door that's more than an inch open. . . we're talking eighteen wheeler semis."

But at the press junket shortly before the film opened, Walter was less hopeful, and in fact stated that he would be just as happy not to read any more reviews of the films which always opened by focusing on the advancing age of the actors. "I don't think we should be condemned as a group and summarily dismissed because of the age factor. I don't want to hear that abuse any more," Koenig stated, but he also had other reasons as to why be believed that *Star Trek VI* would be the final voyage for the original crew. "I think the studio feels that they have an up and coming contender waiting in the wings with the Next Generation.

"They've taken a stand that this is the last picture, not that that stand is irrevocable. But they're thinking now isn't along those terms. In twenty-five years we've done a bang-up job—we've made a whole thing about this being the last voyage. Let's leave it at that. And then there's a certain amount of wish-fulfillment on my part—I'm ready to let go. I'm not fed-up. I'm not over-saturated with *Star Trek.* I'm ready to let go and see if there's anything else out there for me. I'd like to be hungry again. With that little apprehension, with that need comes hopefully some inspiration and some creativity. I've been a little complacent, as a consequence. That doesn't mean that I haven't done anything in the last twenty-five years except *Star Trek,* but there's something to be said for additional motivation for having to feed your family."

Perhaps a bit more sanguine than Koenig, James Doohan has freely admitted that he would never turn down another shot to play Scotty, nor does he believe that this is their last flight together. "There's no way that this is going to be the last, because this film we've just done is a perfect film—absolutely flawless—and there's no reason at all it won't make probably a $150 million, and Paramount is not going to turn that down. I don't care what Bill [Shatner] says. He's going along with the house ruling on that. It's all a big ploy."

Doohan is quite open about his opinions on the Star Trek motion picture series, stating that the sixth one is his favorite, and why.

"Number one got very boring getting to V'ger—it took them twelve minutes to get to V'ger and all they showed us was some thin white clouds. It was terrible. At the preview in Washington, Bill Shatner and I fell asleep. Then in *The Wrath of Khan* the editing was lousy, except for what the director had edited back into the ABC version. The TV version was much better. My part was slashed to bits, and I think I know who to blame for that, but I can't mention his name. Crazy kind of editing. The perfectly edited *Wrath of Khan* was perfect *Star Trek.* Number three was a so-so script. Number four was a great story but not pure *Star Trek.* Number five was just a bad film. Number six is perfect—flawless.